Also by Thordis Simonsen:

YOU MAY PLOW HERE
The Narrative of Sara Brooks

DANCING GIRL

Henry Miller described Greece as a sacred precinct. The motif I created for *Dancing Girl* conveys the spirit of his words. The central star represents God's celestial home. Overlying the star is a personal rendition of a cross that decorates the door of a mountain chapel above my village, Elika. The branched base of the cross roots God—or the deities—in the world of earthlings. Encircling the cross is a field of stars—the dwelling place of all souls.　　　—*T.S.*

Dancing Girl

themes and improvisations in a greek village setting

Thordis Simonsen

The Fundamental Note

Denver

The text in this book is composed in Palatino; display type is set in Novarese. The book is printed on neutral pH paper. Composition by Claudia Previn, Johnson Publishing Company. Film processing and printing by LeRoy Ullmann, The New Lab, and Thordis Simonsen. Reprographics by Artist's Angle, Inc. Manufacturing by Braun–Brumfield, Inc. Cover and book design by Jody Chapel, Cover to Cover Design. Printed in the United States of America.

The Fundamental Note edition first published September, 1991.

Library of Congress Catalog Card Number: 91-72594

ISBN 0-9629766-4-4

The Fundamental Note, P.O. Box 6107, Denver, Colorado 80206
3 4 5 6 7 8 9 0

*Dedicated to the dancers in my family:
my mother Marian and her father, Grandpa Rownd*

celestial navigation

Foul weather
a storm
and
the eye
turns inward.
A tranquil sea
mediterranean turquoise
sparks clarity.
Bright crystals
of light
rise
star-like.
Beacons
in the night
call
the sailor
home.

contents

Acknowledgments   *xi*
Introduction   *xiii*

The Tourista   *1*
The Quintessential Hat   *6*
A Cypress in the Wind   *11*
Maiden Voyage   *13*
The Same Face   *20*
Walking Shoes   *25*
An Open Invitation   *29*
Men's Work   *32*
Eggs, but No Hens   *35*
Lament   *39*
Flying the Horizon   *41*
Mooring   *45*
Telephone Reception   *49*
An Unwelcome Bedfellow   *53*
Martha   *58*
What Became of the Pomegranate   *61*
A Beacon in the Night   *66*
Kotetsi Song   *70*
Karekla   *73*
Long Days' Journey into the Night   *76*
The Kids Get My Goat   *81*

Field Day   85
Much Work, Nothing Else   88
Tasty Bread   95
Here and There   100
Do You Remember the Horse?   107
Orphans   110
A Real Odyssey   118
The Immortal Homer   124
Dancing Girl   130
Good News   137
The Astronomer   141
Homing   144
Spiral Mountain   149
Elika   156
Good Road, Good Life   161
This Blessed House   166
Elikiotissa   172
Initiation   176
Banner Day   182
Dreams and Expectations   186
Halcyon Days   192
Patina   197

acknowledgments

With immense joy I acknowledge the village Elika for embracing my presence; Richard Gooding, my parents, the Cabot Trust, the Elikioton Society, Anne Healy, and Arminta Neal for their generous financial support; Zoe Tsigounis, Yioryia Kolyvodiakos, Eleftheria Kavasila, and Nick Kousoulis for their adept translating; Peggy Mazaraki for her precise transcriptions; Nancy Zeilig, Helen Yeager, and David Kaslow for their sensitive literary counsel; Mihail Tsigounis for his scholarly reading; Linda Bevard for her superlative copy editing; Katy Tartakoff for her compelling photographs; Jody Chapel for her impeccable taste; Claudia Previn and Cindy Young for picking up the beat.

introduction

When I tell people that I live part of each year in Greece, they invariably reply, "Oh, I've *always* wanted to go to Greece!" As if preformed and waiting for the appropriate cue, the statement spills out instantaneously and, by now, predictably. Even so, I start every time at the sound of it because I only vaguely imagined traveling in Greece, and I never foresaw living there. Greece lies south along the Mediterranean, and I am a northerner by descent: my maternal ancestors reputedly arrived on the *Mayflower*, and my father's grandparents immigrated from Norway. I have always identified most closely with my Norwegian heritage because my name is Norwegian and because the family connection is more recent—a cousin of mine lives in Oslo today. Norway was the first country I visited abroad, and before going to Greece I had traveled in Northern Europe exclusively.

Of course, when people learn that Greece is my foster homeland, they ask, "Why did you choose to live in Greece?" I always think to myself, I don't know! I didn't! Had I planned to live abroad, I would have traded Scandinavia's latitude for a village nested high in the Alps. But before my perplexed expression and unuttered words cause alarm, I simply explain how I got to Greece in the first place.

In 1974 when I wanted a village experience to draw upon in my anthropology teaching, I contacted Zoe, a first cousin of a Greek-American friend of mine. Zoe had married in Elika, her father's village. I knew she would arrange a room for me to rent and would help me out were I to stumble into difficulty in a country where I could not speak the language.

Oh, I knew enough about Greece to yearn like everyone else to go there. My Greek-American friend had painted an enticing picture, which her mother's radiant warmth and crispy cheese pies confirmed. But the mystical quality of my Elika experience makes the means of my arrival difficult to comprehend, let alone explain. And so I tell inquirers that I selected my sunlit, sea-level village located at the southern-most reach of Greece as much for convenience as by intent.

Logic equally dominates the explanation of my return to Elika in 1981. I went back because I had been before, and not, certainly, with an eye toward settling there. More than anything I wanted to say hello to Thea, my first landlady and friend, because I had not seen her to bid her farewell before departing seven years earlier. Looming on the horizon of my memory, this omission drew me back—not the lure of rocking to sea on a donkey's back or walking along ancient stone footpaths into the hills.

During my seven years away, Elika had busied herself changing from a primarily subsistence-oriented economy based on animal and hand power to a cash economy based on gasoline. Motorized irrigation pumps, tractors, and other four-wheeled vehicles had appeared, along with conspicuously new habits, values, and relationships. Meanwhile, during the same seven years, I had busied myself teaching my high school anthropology course and interviewing, editing, and photographing in conjunction with my first book, *You May Plow Here: The Narrative of Sara Brooks.* The anthropology course gave me the interest in documenting Elika's transformation, and the book project gave me the skills.

So in the fall of 1982 I placed my beloved cat in a carefully chosen foster home, I sold my middle-aged car, I put my profuse belongings into storage, and, with a grant from the Cabot Trust in my pocket, I moved to Elika. Zoe, the same woman who had found me a room to rent during my two earlier visits, found a house for me to occupy indefinitely. I intended to create a book-length portrait of Elika comprised of photographs and interviews with villagers. I assumed the interviews would be conducted with the assistance of translators since I barely spoke Greek, but they seldom materialized, and old folks who would have been key participants in a village narrative one by one "went traveling" before I could immortalize them on tape. I was despondent.

Then I read Zora Neale Hurston's *Mules and Men,* which suggested to me that the documentarian's story could enhance the document. Over time I stretched a good idea to its extreme: I decided to let the story of my life in Elika *be* the document. Not surprising, in retrospect, because I went to live in Elika as much to test new values I had adopted during my anthropology teaching as to observe and record village life.

But *Dancing Girl* wants to be more than a chronicle of personal experiences. The book wants to lay out what I have learned in Greece, which accounts for why I have spent so much time in Elika—at least part of every year since 1981— and why I bought and am restoring an abandoned peasant house there. In other words, *Dancing Girl* promises to answer the question raised earlier: why did you choose to live in Greece? The Mediterranean light inspires me, but my intuition tells me I chose Greece in order to navigate her starlit night sky.

DANCING GIRL

the tourista

On July the Fourth, 1974, I taxied for the first time from the ancient port town, Monemvasia, to my destination village, Elika. I didn't speak any Greek, so I engaged a car by parroting my village name to every prospective driver in sight. Finally a zealous bystander pointed me toward a stale gray sedan parked nearby. Echoes of "Elika, Elika, Elika!" emanating from within drew me close, and when the driver opened a back door, the already settled passengers waved me in.

But the capacity of the vehicle had already been stretched by people and parcels—Greeks travel with an abundance of parcels. In them villagers carry every conceivable fresh agricultural product in season to their relatives in Athina (Athens) and abroad: olive oil, head cheese, greens, oranges, fish, fragile tomatoes, and even delicate eggs! I can picture one traveler who, I am told, departed from Elika with a wheelbarrow load of luggage and even then staggered under the weight of overstuffed *tagaria* (woven sacks) hung on her shoulders!

When Greeks return to their villages, they carry similar containers repacked with small appliances, yardage, shoes, confections, and other commercially produced goods for their own and other village households. A generation ago, I have learned, they brought clothing by the trunkful: fifty suits, fifty shirts, fifty neckties, as many sets of underwear and pairs of socks for the men, and dozens of sets of clothing for their wives, too. With innumerable swollen cartons and valises, my awaiting co-travelers followed tradition. I squeezed into a full car with my own bag—Greeks always make room for one more—and a bulging taxi lumbered off.

We were traveling in the state of Lakonia in the Peloponnese. The word *kolpos* means "gulf" and "bosom," and the Lakonian Gulf divides the southern half of the state into two pendulous peninsulas. Monemvasia, "the Gibraltar of Greece," crowns the east coast of the eastern peninsula. Elika sits three kilometers off the southwest coast of the same peninsula.

The fastest if not shortest route between Monemvasia and Elika is a thirty-three-kilometer section of two-lane asphalt road. For the duration of our drive, my Greek co-passengers stared wide-eyed at my strangeness—a phenomenon I was to experience for some time in Elika as well. I am not self-conscious when I escape style-bound middle-class America, so I wondered what accounted for the bold, almost rudely satisfied curiosity about me. Years later in Norway I faced large audiences of students who mirrored back the blond thatch and blue eyes I inherited from my father's Norwegian grandparents, and I understood why my appearance engaged these dark-complexioned, dark-haired, dark-eyed Greeks.

I had reached Monemvasia from Athina by overnight ferry, so while my traveling companions fixed their gazes on me, the features of the landscape held my attention. We rolled over expansive, voluptuous hills—fitting counterparts to the Taiyetos Mountains, a series of impressive brawny peaks running the length of our twin peninsula, the Mani, which is sometimes visible across the gulf.

Although graceful, the hills we traversed are unrefined, unembellished. Walled terraces, citrus groves, vineyards, and single-crop vegetable fields impose an order on the land where they exist, but local agriculture, based primarily on the olive, occurs predominantly "in the wild" alongside scattered lobe-leafed figs, almonds, redolent carobs, walnuts, and of course cypress spires. These cast their shadows on patches of cultivated wheat that compete with every variety of thorny undergrowth and sweet-smelling herb. Behold, a landscape textured in green and gold. Untamed, her beauty could not be foretold.

Gifts held secret, and the people who would facilitate their disclosure, were nowhere visible. As is customary during the summer *mesimeri* (midday), villagers had deserted their land, the road, and the men their *cafenia* (coffee houses) in favor of cool whitewashed interiors of red clay tile–roofed houses. Because no relatives or friends were in sight to stop us along the way, our taxi transported us to Elika without interruption at speeds automobiles were designed to sustain— my companions silently crossing themselves in response to standing ikons dotting the roadside.

I arrived in Elika within an hour and was delivered to Thea, a vigorous though not fastidious woman from whom I rented a room for several weeks—the duration of my first stay in the village. Undecorated and furnished with little more than a narrow uneven bed and a straight chair, my quarters were Spartan and somewhat uncomfortable, especially because a "modern" concrete slab roof radiated stored heat into the room at night. But a deep magenta bougainvillea clung to my balcony, from which I viewed church dome, rooftops, descending hills, and a protracted sea.

When the afternoon cooled, I explored my immediate neighborhood briefly and then joined the Tsigounises, my contact family, for the first of innumerable delightful meals. Zoe is a Greek-American who married in Elika in 1958. Her Greek husband Mihail speaks English flawlessly. Both have shared invaluable facts and insights about life in Elika, as well as gossip about me—"the Tourista"—during frequent extended conversations. But this evening Zoe packed me off early—with *paksimadhia* (twice-baked bread), an orange, and an almond paste sweet for breakfast.

As a full moon rose over the mountains, I returned to Thea. She welcomed me and tendered her friendship with the fragrant pink carnation she presented me on my way in. (Appreciatively I displayed it in a buttonhole the next day.) I said goodnight and thought I had taken my leave of Thea when I entered my room, but she had trailed in behind me. Speaking words I could not comprehend, she made a beeline for my balcony shutters, which she closed ceremoniously. Eager not to obstruct the inward drift of cool night air—and assuming it a matter of preference—I reopened the shutters in her presence. She stepped closer to me and repeated her message more loudly so as to make herself understood and then reclosed the shutters decisively. When I gestured my acquiescence, we confirmed our mutual agreement with the two words common to our different vocabularies: all right! Eventually I learned from Zoe that my landlady had urged me to latch the shutters at night and to call her "Thea"—Aunt—to deter the man, a stranger, who rented a room next to mine!

Exhilarated and exhausted by my introduction to Elika, I went straight to bed—after once again very quietly unlatching the shutters. At daybreak I would be awakened by worry beads clicking in the hands of men—soon off to their fields—drinking coffee in the *cafenio* below my balcony. But I passed the night at ease, embraced by Elika, the wet nurse of my second upbringing.

the quintessential hat

A staccato of sound! Thea's insistent rapping on my door vaguely impressed me, but I remained dormant until an odious thought spurred me into action: every minute I wasted now would prolong Thea's and my homeward journey under a mid-July afternoon sun so hot it bakes bread. I dressed quickly, ate lightly, grabbed my camera and my hat, and shot out the door.

Thea had cinched two packsaddles and was standing by. I arrived eager to mount up and head out, but I hesitated, not knowing whether I was to ride the donkey or the horse. Furthermore, I wasn't sure how to get on. Neither of the packsaddles was equipped with stirrups—Greeks don't rely on costly, cumbersome, complex, man-made devices when natural aids are at hand. Thea simply led the animals to a nearby rock, nudged them broadside, stepped onto the ready mounting block, and settled onto the donkey. Following her example, I got on the horse.

Within minutes of my four-twenty-a.m. wake-up call, we were on our way—Thea proceeding on her nameless sleepy bay with large ears and short legs, and me atop Psari, a tall, wide-eyed creature whose silver-speckled hide resembled the underside of a fish. (The name Psari means "fish-color.") In no time we traveled beyond the reach of spotty village streetlights and penetrated the darkness—a crescent moon overhead provided companionship, but no light. Thea navigated unerringly, nevertheless. A matchmaker in former years, she had attended engagement celebrations in nearby mountain villages, and—riding my Psari alone at midnight under a moonless sky—she always found her way home to Elika.

We were now climbing to the village Koulentia where Thea would visit her mother's sister, Maria. I thought I was just going along for the ride, but this journey, on my twelfth day in Elika, turned into an initiation.

Around daybreak we reached Pandanassa. Viewed from her sister village, Elika, she resembles chalk marks penciled on a distant hillside. But close up, this village is a typical cluster of textured stucco houses brightened by colorful window shutters and softened by draping grapevines—another arena for life, both sacred and mundane. By the time we arrived in Pandanassa, the customary early morning farmyard racket had roused the villagers from sleep, but they had not appeared on the street. We passed through without halting.

The sun's warmth reached into even the lowest dips and pockets as we made our way up to the next community, Yeroumana. When we arrived, men had populated the *cafenio*, but the particular fellow Thea had set her heart on finding was not among them. When she asked for him by name, she learned that he had gone to Neapolis (a market town twenty-five kilometers from Elika) for the day. She was crestfallen.

Rumor had it that I took special delight in photographing moustached men. Aware of this, the men in Elika had been preening for my camera. And Thea had planned to surprise me with the opportunity to photograph this man from her home village who trimmed an exceptionally handsome moustache. When she appealed for a substitute, no one appeared.

I tried to let Thea know how much I appreciated her thoughtfulness while assuring her that I was not overwhelmingly disappointed. But a determination that has taken her where other women fear to tread—in concert with God's will—ultimately produced a subject. Outside Yeroumana we stopped at Ay Lia, a mountain chapel distinguished by a bell hung in a large nearby tree. Thea entered the chapel and lit a candle before we continued toward Koulentia. When we arrived at the village *agora* (market place), Thea once again made her appeal for a moustached face. A suitable subject materialized instantaneously. When I clicked the shutter, I obliged Thea *and* the man's friends who had good-humoredly dragged him to my camera from his observer's seat on the sidewalk outside the *cafenio*.

Having at last dispensed with Thea's first order of business, we made our way to her aunt Maria's. The priest Papa Nikolas had taken Maria at age ten as his wife; then he went away to Asia Minor to participate in Greece's war against Turkey (which ended in 1922 with the Asia Minor Catastrophe). Papa Nikolas' captors nailed horseshoes to the soles of his feet and hung him from a tree. His unfulfilled widow fell in love with another man who, laughing, refused her. Struck with remorse for her dead husband, Maria sold her dowry land and built a small chapel where, cloistering herself, she worked for God and begged His forgiveness. Thea liked to visit her aunt periodically; she furnished Maria with some garden produce and oil for her lamps.

I don't remember the woman herself, and at that time I would not have understood the conversation. But I never will forget how much at home I felt in the little chapel, Ay Nikolas. An array of yellow stars danced on an arched, daylight blue ceiling overhead.

Rejuvenated by our late morning intermission at the chapel, I was happy to be trailing homeward with my sidekick, Thea. The afternoon sun glared, so she pulled her dark scarf lower across her forehead, and I put on my sunglasses. And my hat—a broad-brimmed, high-crowned, brown-and-tan patterned straw hat. I tied it down against a strong current, but the wind's deft fingers snatched the hat and carried it off. Thea must have anticipated the trouble. She slid to the ground and overtook my hat before I had begun to react. She gave it to me and remounted from the closest rock. As a result of this display, my already considerable appreciation for Thea increased dramatically. Here was a woman who demonstrated the acuity of a scout, the command of a wagon master, the stamina of a teamster, and the spunk of a school-age kid.

Repossessing my hat, I retied it, but with cunning and punch, the trickster wind eventually stole it again. This time, to save Thea, I made sure *I* did the rescuing. I dropped to the ground and pounced on my hat. Like Thea, I had outmatched the wind!

Now to remount. My Psari was a long-legged horse, and the packsaddle was high up. I saw an opportunity, and I leapt for it. Instead of leading the horse to the nearest rock for a step up, I took a running jump and landed on the seat. "Bravo," Thea applauded. Cowgirl fashion, I yipped and whooped the rest of the way home. Thea joined in with songs and whistles. And our mounts quickened their pace.

Zoe laughed and pointed at me in surprise when I appeared at her door sometime after our early afternoon return. She said the villagers had calculated that the mighty *vorias* (north wind) that day would sweep me away with my hat. My wiry appearance concerns them, and the women always fill up my plate—three delicate *kourambiedhes* (almond cookies) instead of one or a heap of macaroni large enough to serve everyone at the table. "Don't fear!" they admonish. "Eat. Eat so you will fatten."

My lack of weight notwithstanding, I came home from Koulentia with my hat.

a cypress in the wind

A salt-and-pepper tail swished across Psari's rump, which swayed in front of me as Thea—mounted on her horse—and I—on foot—climbed the steep mountain trail to Skopeles. Her husband Manolis, a tall, white-haired man of considerable girth, had ridden ahead on the diminutive donkey, which accounts for the fact that for this outing I relied on my own footing and vitality—adequate, Thea estimated, given my gymnastic display on our return from Koulentia a few days earlier. At Skopeles, Thea and Manolis, along with most villagers, owned a parcel of land. Irrigating with cold spring water, they raised onions, tomatoes, beans, squash, and melon for their own consumption, as well as wheat for bread and feed for Psari and the donkey.

It was July, and throughout the hills wild and hand-sown grains had ripened and dried. Endless streams of glistening black ants, clasping spiked kernels, wore paths to their nests. And villagers, leading animals loaded with wheat, converged on Elika's one threshing lot. There, during the established week, a mammoth vibrating machine with conveyors, chutes, belts, and rollers separated the seed from the chaff before they were bagged and baled.

By the time Thea and I arrived at Skopeles, Manolis had already lashed six bundles of wheat onto the donkey. Dwarfed by a bulky cargo, the uncomplaining freighter waited. Thea dismounted and muzzled Psari with a red-and-black checkered *tagari* employed as a feed bag. Meanwhile Manolis dipped his fingers into a cup of water and splattered the heads of the wheat Psari would carry. Then, with a seaman's artistry, he roped three bundles—heads down—on each side of the packsaddle.

Wheat stubble poking up all around trilled in the morning light. Too wise to linger, Thea and I and her obedient team filed back down the much traveled path to Elika. Dampened and inverted, the precious grain heads traveled safely, in spite of grabby trailside branches.

We went directly to the threshing field, which lay beside the main road just east of Elika. There, domes the color of anthills rose up as the villagers, day by day, stacked on more and more rounds of hay. Refusing my help as always, Thea undertook her work without pause. A long-sleeved aquamarine cotton outer shirt protected her arms from the twelve bundles of bristly wheat, which she released one at a time by a tug on the rope and maneuvered onto her lofty pile.

Aged sixty-one, Thea stood up to her work silently, almost obstinately—like the unassailable cypress tree confronting the wind god Boreas. She worked like a man, and not one iota of shame clouded dark eyes sparkling with the clarity of spring water.

maiden voyage

In 1938 at age twenty-four, Krisoula Mihalis Favas donned her wedding dress and married thirty-eight-year-old Emmanouil Zaharias Manolitsis. Because Krisoula—my friend Thea—was more daring, more clever, more industrious, and—although she never said so—more beautiful than other maidens, she had many suitors. Each presented his qualifications and stated his dowry requirements through his appointed matchmaker, often a relative. Thea's father had died when she was eight years old, so her father's brother, Uncle Dhemosthenis Favas, represented her. When Manolis' family accepted the promise of forty thousand drachmas in dowry, Thea's mother wed her off.

Like other girls of her day, Thea began preparing her dowry when she was fifteen. During the summer months when the olives were producing fruit and there were fewer demands on her time, Thea often slaved deep into the night with only the dim light of a small olive oil lamp. She loomed rugs, blankets, and indigo plaid bed sheets, as well as fabric for pillowcases, tablecloths, towels, and clothing which she sewed and hand decorated. In addition, with the money she earned picking figs at Asopos and Kalivia, she purchased thick blankets and fine sheets at church festivals.

During the first three days of Thea's wedding week, in keeping with tradition, she washed and pressed her dowry and helped bake sweets, including bridal white *kourambiedhes*. Song lightened the weight of her iron; song sweetened the taste of her pastries.

On Thursday at midday, violins announced the arrival of the groom and his friends, who had traveled the two hours by horse from Elika to Thea's village Yeroumana. At Thea's house, everyone celebrated around trays of appetizers and sweets before Thea's older brother Yiorgos read the inventory of the dowry the groom had come to collect. Eventually, two trunks covered with white hand-embroidered cloths and four equally beautifully wrapped and tied bundles were loaded on packsaddles blanketed in vibrant red, green, and yellow. By evening the dowry had been transported and deposited at the groom's father's house in Elika, and the taps of wine barrels had been opened. Everyone danced "as late into the night as they had courage."

On Friday at midday, Manolis and a dozen friends again arrived at Thea's house. With more festivity, Manolis claimed the bride's undergarments and nightgown—her *poukamiso*—and sweets, and carried them back to Elika.

On Saturday, lambs and goats both in Elika and Yeroumana were slaughtered and butchered to be baked on Sunday. On Saturday evening, the bride's family gathered at the bride's house and feasted; the groom's family gathered at the groom's house and did likewise. Every evening all week long, both families had celebrated: food and wine, violins, song and dance.

On Sunday, Thea married. Traditionally the bride married in white, whether a seamstress custom-fashioned the dress or the bride's family rented a gown from a store in Neapolis or from the church in Elika. (For a few hundred drachmas, families could rent a lovely gown that relatives in America had sent to the church for that purpose.)

On *her* wedding day, Thea wore a beautiful dress a seamstress had sewn from fabric Manolis had chosen and purchased in Neapolis, along with undergarments, stockings, shoes, and jewelry—his engagement gifts. Thea had already worn the dress once before at the celebration of her engagement. With nine children in her family and no father to contribute to their support, Thea's mother could not afford the price of fabric for a wedding gown, and Manolis furnished none. So Thea cast off into matrimony outfitted in rose.

The wedding was held at Yeroumana. Before the ceremony, the guests gathered outside the Favas' olive factory and feasted. Throughout the winter nights of her maidenhood, after picking olives all day long, Thea—alongside her brother—had pressed her shoulder into the wooden bar that turned the olive oil press. On her wedding day, the factory doors became banquet tables; on them Thea's family laid out a meal prepared by Thea and a host of other women over a period of days. Because the Favases were poor, the abundance of food on the tables "terrified" the guests: winter melon, *pastitsio* and other baked dishes, potatoes, fish.

After the meal, the priest crowned the betrothed with the traditional wedding wreaths. Then Yiorgos counted the money arriving guests had strewn, along with gifts, on the banquet tables. Finally, a cavalcade of horses escorted the married couple to Elika where the groom's family hosted a second feast. Mounted on white horses and sitting on packsaddles blanketed in white, Thea and Manolis pranced off in a shower of confetti, money, flowers, and rice. Behind them, ten cavaliers carried as many beautifully crafted baskets containing the wedding gifts. All in all, one hundred horses trotted in a parade animated by music, song, and a chorus of good wishes: good life; good fortune.

At the groom's house, wine glasses continued to clink and dancers continued to circle when the wedding couple finally retired to their bedchamber. Traditionally when a husband and wife consummated their marriage on their wedding night, she dressed in her white cotton *poukamiso* and lay in bed with it arranged under her so that she could present it, blood stained, to her mother-in-law the next morning. When the mother-in-law saw the "sign" on the *poukamiso*, she reported the news to her family. In Elika, the groom's father or brother or the groom himself fired gunshots, which invited more gift-giving and initiated another week of celebration.

If the *poukamiso* was unmarked, the bride's in-laws became enraged and drove her back to her father's house. Thea remembered one bride from Koulentia who was not "okay," and to vindicate her, her sister said, "Remember, Stavroula, when the black bull butted you with its horn?" It was a true story; in the end, the girl's family paid a higher dowry sum, and the in-laws kept her.

But if a larger dowry payment did not appease the in-laws, the unchaste girl remained home, a single divorcee for the rest of her life. So mothers agonized that their daughters remain virgins, and girls exercised extreme caution. So much value was placed on the *poukamiso*—the "price"—that a woman kept it and wore it to her grave. "Now," Thea explained, "girls can take the pill, do what they want, and never become pregnant. Today the girls are no more cautious than the boys. And now," Thea agonized, "when girls do become pregnant they go to the hospitals, abort their babies, and throw them in the trash!" By contrast, when an unmarried contemporary of Thea's became pregnant, she went away and gave birth without identifying the father. After two days, her brother found her, took the baby from her breast, and killed it. He believed that because his unwed sister was not a virgin, she must be a whore. He killed out of shame; he was never brought to justice.

On her wedding night Thea wore the customary *poukamiso*, stitched by a seamstress. But she had no mother-in-law to claim the price, and when her sister-in-law came to verify her virginity, Thea exclaimed, "What thing is this to arrive in order to make verification!" And she let her husband know how displeased she was. Her sister-in-law never saw the *poukamiso*. Thea trimmed her sail; she navigated uncharted waters.

■

In 1990, Thea's twenty-five-year-old granddaughter, Maria Lambi Houlis, married according to modified tradition. Maria is the daughter of the Lambi Houlis from whom I purchased my house. She married a Neapolis boy she began dating in junior high school. Matchmakers were not required. Maria's dowry included a parcel of land, an apartment in Athina, a university education, and her gymnastics school in Neapolis.

Maria prepared for her wedding for weeks. On Thursday of her wedding week, family and friends threw gifts and one-thousand-drachma notes on a bed at the groom's house in Neapolis. *Kourambiedhes* were served.

Before the ceremony on Saturday, a relative of the groom went to Maria's house in Elika and inconspicuously claimed Maria's undergarments—no *poukamiso*. He unceremoniously delivered them to the groom's house after the wedding.

On Saturday afternoon, Maria was married in Elika. I went to her house before the ceremony and found a host of sedate, well-dressed men and women from Elika, Neapolis, and abroad. I ate the *kourambiedhes* I was served and then, on Lambi's urging, I went into the bridal chamber to salute the bride. Maria was dressed in an elegant white gown rented in Athina for one hundred thousand drachmas. She was posing for a video camera. Not wishing to intrude, I turned and mingled with the other guests.

Shortly Maria, escorted by her handsomely suited father, stepped out of the house and led the wedding procession down the street to the church. Two precious flower girls carried Maria's train. The procession grew as people joined in along the way. Other villagers waved from verandas.

And from the threshold of Maria's house all the way to the church gate, a voice rose up above the hum of the crowd. In an attempt to inflame the wedding party with a depth of human feeling only music—and dance—can inspire, Thea sang out.

Comb our bride; take the combings
And send them to the jeweler to make a ring.

They are taking our partridge with the golden plumes,
And they are leaving our neighborhood with sadness.
Neighbors, neighbors, your neighbor is gone—
Among all, most beautiful and your chieftess.

Thea clapped, Thea danced, and Thea sang without pause. Insistently, persistently—alone. A mutiny at sea.

After the church ceremony, guests received white candied almonds tied in netting. The wedding pair, traveling in a polished, flower-bedecked sedan, sped—horns blowing—to Neapolis. There the groom's family hosted a lavish wedding feast. Ten circles danced traditional songs played on electric instruments. Both the bride's and the groom's families and their guests celebrated late into the night—long after the married couple had slipped away.

■

I saw Thea a few weeks after Maria's wedding. She was still glowing with pleasure from the wedding videotapes she had viewed two days before. "Thea, why wouldn't the other women sing?" I asked. "They wouldn't open their mouths," she said. "The girls are ashamed to sing now. Likewise when someone dies, they are ashamed to sing the dirges. I don't think it's beautiful not to cry from sorrow and not to rejoice with pleasure." "Thea," I wanted to know, "what gave you the courage to continue?" "Maria was my first granddaughter to marry," she explained.

the same face

The maiden, Thea, once accompanied an aunt to the festival at Elika's church, Ay Haralambos. By coincidence, they sat at Manolis Manolitsis' table. When Manolis treated them, Thea raised her glass and toasted him, "To your health." At the time, she knew he was engaged, but she did not know he had been matched to her. When she did learn, she accepted him. She could see that he was manly and handsome, and people said he was a landowner and a good husband. He was a widower; his first wife had died from heartbreak after fever had taken their two young sons.

Thea gave Manolis five healthy children—the first born in 1940, another in 1942, the third in 1945, and two more following in rapid succession. Because she began raising her family during a decade of military occupation and civil war (the German–Italian Occupation from 1941 to 1944; the Civil War from 1946 to 1949), Thea's life as a mother was a great struggle. She couldn't buy meat or milk. What milk the family had they consumed warm from the goat, unsweetened, with mouthfuls of sodden bread. This was not so different from Thea's own childhood, when she squirted milk from the goat directly onto her bread and ate it.

During the forties wheat was scarce—two kilos cost an entire day's wage—so Thea baked bread from unsifted barley flour. But the bread was so unappealing that she often went to her mother's mill in Yeroumana. Her mother operated the mill that had been her husband's, and she gave Thea ten or fifteen kilos of flour to make wheat bread. Other times Mihail's father, Theodhoros Tsigounis, lent her wheat flour. He sowed many fields, and he had in abundance.

In those years, the olive oil ran out because Thea's trees at that time only produced two or three hundred kilos of oil. One year, she made only twenty kilos of oil, so she borrowed from Tsigounis. Thea paid him back when she could, but he never asked for interest. In fact, he gave gratuitously to those in dire need so the children would not die of hunger. Tsigounis was a good soul.

When the war years ended, Thea continued to suffer because her husband did not live up to expectation. Before she married him, she observed his strength, and she believed the words of her uncle Dhemosthenis' wife, who had told Thea that Manolis had made three thousand kilos of oil. Later she learned that he had not even made one hundred.

Manolis turned out to be derelict. He didn't care about anything except to drink wine at the *taverna* and for Thea to have his food ready. He did not take an interest in whether the children went to school or whether Thea made their three daughters' dowries. And when Thea built their new house, he never searched for a single worker; he didn't carry so much as two barrels of water to wet down the concrete; he didn't buy any wine for the workers. Even when Thea found him day's work, he wouldn't go by himself. Only when they went to the fields together, Manolis worked diligently and beautifully. Then he did the work of three men.

When Thea demanded Manolis' help, she became the object of criticism from the other women and men—especially the men. Manolis went to the *taverna* in the morning, and he sat there until midnight if Thea did not retrieve him. When she did enter the *taverna*, his friends goaded him, "Your wife will make you do whatever she wants." In response, Manolis hurled insults at her and often refused to budge. The men scoffed at Thea because at that time the *taverna* was strictly a male domain, yet she dared go inside. They seemed to take pleasure in the fact that her children were hungry and suffered while Manolis sat and gave them company. Finally, for revenge, so she wouldn't go into the *taverna*, the men called her "Esa." (*ESA* is the acronym for *Elliniki Stratiotiki Astinomia*, the Hellenic Military Police.) "I took it very hard," Thea frowned.

Thea was stronger than many men, and she worked extra hard to compensate for her husband's negligence. Consequently, she had little time to be neighborly and gossip. Behind her back, the women accused her of inferior housekeeping because she kept potatoes and olives in the house—she didn't have a storeroom then. And since she was always away, they asked among themselves when she would stay home and make her daughters' dowries. When they saw the dowries, however, "they rubbed their eyes and said nothing."

"I sat in a different seat," Thea explained. If she had entirely avoided the *taverna*, and if she had conformed to the other women's traditional housekeeping standards, the neighbor men and women would not have rebuked her. "People criticized me because I was the manager, and I looked after everything," Thea lamented. "But I didn't want to give them the satisfaction of seeing my family go hungry."

Sober, Manolis always regretted the foul language he spoke in drunkenness. When his children grew up, he went to work with them, and in that way, little by little, he stopped drinking wine. Now Thea is a widow, and her children have married and are raising families of their own. But Thea continues to work hard, and even though she keeps her mind on her own business and does not judge "where one and another goes and what one and another does," she still draws criticism—she walks across the *agora* in her work clothes.

In the old days, people returned from the fields in the clothes they had worked in. They washed them at home, but they were patched. In those days, people patched their clothes; they did not throw them away. Back then, people used to tell the story about one woman who was lazy; when her clothes were covered with patches, she didn't make new ones. "You don't go to church," villagers said. "No," she replied, "I don't have any clothes." So everyone gave her something—a dress, shoes. She went to church, and just as the liturgy ended, one woman took back her dress, another woman took back something else. Naked, the lazy woman ran to her house and began to weave clothes.

Before Thea married, her mother sent her younger sister to sell some veal. She wore a hand-loomed dress with a monstrous patch in the back. An American man, who had arrived with a large sum of money, met her. He wanted to marry her. Because her mother had two older daughters to wed, she did not let her go. But the wealthy American had paid attention to her and had solicited her hand in marriage—even though she wore a patched dress.

Over time the villagers have seen more and more wealthy Athenians and Americans dressing up and showing off. According to Thea, the villagers think this is a beautiful thing. Consequently, they don't wear patched clothes at all any more. And they wear a clean set of clothes to work—not church clothes—and they change into old clothes at the field. They do this so they can be dressed cleanly when they return to the village. When her neighbors continue to see Thea walking across the *agora* in her dusty work clothes, they snicker, "See the filthy woman." But Thea contends, "Whether one wears work clothes or clean clothes, it's the same face."

walking shoes

One day in 1982, I was walking the Marathia road. Distress cries drew my attention to an approaching pickup. There in the cargo bin, in the company of household goods and gardening tools, stood a white, frightened goat. Whether the goat was more scared of the vehicle or the operator, I cannot say, although we all know the terror of riding with an inexperienced driver. And in 1982, drivers in Elika were learners—except one. That was Mihail, the village president. He had owned a pickup for years—Elika's first pickup, and first sedan and tractor, too. Mihail was a pacesetter in his community. And Mihail's father owned a goat. But Theodhoros set an example; he never allowed his son to transport his goat in the truck. Even in his advanced years—he lived into his nineties—he walked his goat in order to move it from here to there.

Without a doubt the idea of a goat riding in a truck seems incongruous: goats walk; they don't ride. This goat was miserable; it expected more of its owner. My sympathy lay with the goat: I prefer, also, to walk rather than to ride.

But when I arrived in Elika in 1982, I was as much a victim of circumstance as the goat. I knew in advance that Zoe had arranged for me to rent a small house. I was not forewarned that my tenancy obligated me to chauffeur my landlady's husband, Kyriakos. This seems like a small price to guarantee a roof over my head, but I had sold my own car to come to Greece, and I had really hoped to navigate on foot.

But Kyriakos was in a fix. Two years earlier, with merchant marine income, his oldest son had purchased a teal blue Toyota. At that time—basing the action on an excessively optimistic belief that at least one of his three sons would always be available in Elika to drive the vehicle— Kyriakos gave up his donkey. Whether this was before or after he failed the driving tests, I can't say, but Kyriakos himself was not eligible to drive. When I arrived, none of his sons was home to drive for him. And his daughter-in-law didn't drive because village women had not as yet awakened to the possibility of driving. And whether a matter of pride or exertion, I can't say, but Kyriakos really did not like to walk. And his gardens were still just as far away as they ever had been and required uninterrupted attention; the schedule of plowing and planting and cultivating and harvesting obviously operated independently from his sons' arrivals and departures.

All this made my appearance quite timely, at least as far as Kyriakos was concerned. I was summoned to drive the pickup the day after my arrival in Elika. Mid-morning we headed west along the two-lane highway out of the village and then turned onto an unpaved farm road that took us over a hill and down to his land some three kilometers away. Dressed as he was in clean black leather street shoes and fresh designer denims and a shirt, Kyriakos set to work immediately. With neither indifference nor gaiety, he quickly fed the dogs and chickens, and then he gathered beans, tomatoes, eggplant, figs, and grapes. As he loaded the produce into the truck, he set aside a portion of all but the beans for me to take home myself. And in no time he had climbed back into the cab beside me, and we were on our way back to the village. With the pickup to shuttle us to and from his fields, we accomplished the whole job in less time than a one-way trip on a donkey would have consumed. In addition to the time saved, Kyriakos earned the distinction of being the only man in Elika with a chauffeur, and, rumor had it, his chauffeur was more beautiful than had ever been assigned to any army general.

I was flattered by the compliments attached to my seemingly enviable assignment. And I was pleased to help Kyriakos out, because as a newcomer I had few opportunities to reciprocate village hospitality. But I was relieved when a returning son repossessed the Toyota's ignition key. After that the villagers became accustomed to my penchant for walking; now I can wave them past when they see me on the road because they have learned that time of day, temperature, or season notwithstanding, I am likely to decline a lift.

I made an exception my first day olive picking with Yiannis Papadhakis, his youngest brother Mihalis, and his wife and two sisters-in-law. Out of duty or preference—I do not know which—Yiorgos, the middle brother, would stay home to tend the family *bakaliko/taverna* next door to Thea's. (A *bakaliko* is a general store.) We were to leave from the street in front of the store at eight o'clock in the morning.

I arrived early enough to watch the group assemble— five Papadhakises, their mounts, and an assortment of goats. At the appointed hour Yiorgos emerged from the store and set on the pavement a typical reed-seated straight chair with PAPADHAKIS carved across the top. Starting with the senior Papadhakis, each led his or her donkey up to the chair, which Yiorgos held steady while they launched their bulk—sometimes sizeable—onto their saddles.

Only Garifalia, Yiorgos' wife, did not participate in the ritual. Like Kyriakos, she had abandoned her donkey with the advent of motorcars. But there was no vehicle in her own family, so when the rest of the group headed out of Elika toward the mountain road cutting east, Garifalia walked the short distance down to the main road where she could take advantage of local traffic. I stayed with her, not so much because she too was on foot, but because she, more than the others, embraced my presence.

At the highway, Garifalia stopped a car driving east. We got out at the Ay Mammas road, which we followed a short distance uphill before turning onto the two-track trail to the Papadhakis field house and trees. Shortly after we arrived, the rest of the party appeared, and we worked through a springlike December day while the yearling goats flashed back and forth through the trees.

At the end of the day, Garifalia traveled back to Elika by auto-stop. I chose to accompany the others, along with the livestock, on foot. The camaraderie and relaxed pace of that forty-minute promenade enriched my day. I had chosen well. Irini, my Greek *yiayia* (grandmother), once commented that when she was young and worked, she walked, but without shoes. Now, she observed, everyone has shoes, and no one walks.

I have shoes, and I walk.

an open invitation

A heyday of thistles, a squawky gray gate, battered bare shutters, spattered window glass, springy floorboards, leak-streaked walls, and a host of uninvited guests. The house I rented in Elika reeked neglect.

One fireplace to warm two rooms and a hall, a single cold water spigot in the kitchen, a Turkish facility in an out-building, and a committee of three naked lightbulbs greeted me.

I did not anticipate that my efforts to transform this essentially unimproved house into a home would kindle my own necessary transfiguration—and provoke one action too embarrassing to remember and too ridiculous to forget.

My living quarters occupied the second floor, above a storeroom. Before taking occupancy, I first cleared the way from the road to the outside stairway and from the stairs to the outbuilding. The hardware store in Neapolis does not stock mowing implements, so I uprooted the conspiracy of undergrowth with a mattock. Curious about the foreigner, the neighbor women tracked each rise and fall of the blade, my bending and straightening, pulling and scraping. Entangled in a web of scrutiny, I conjured in my imagination a hedge, a fence, a wall—anything to free me.

I retreated to the outbuilding and, again using the mattock, I raked a straw mat—nesting for snakes—off the concrete floor. Although a Turkish fixture lay in the corner, I saw in my mind's eye glistening white porcelain. But squatting over the hole in the terrazzo slab and ferrying water from the house improved my constitution, and somnambulating under the constellations sharpened my night vision. I learned to open the outhouse door warily, and I smiled, unruffled, at the transient boarders—bats, stray cats, and ferrets—that sometimes glanced by me as I entered. When I moved from the rental, I bade farewell to the Turkish facility and took with me its counterpart, a cobalt blue enamel *yoyo* (chamber pot) I had purchased with trepidation. It helps me weather many storms.

I carried water to the outhouse from an outdoor spigot at ground level at the corner of my house nearest the road. With no bathing facilities inside, I determined to wash at this faucet. I wore a skimpy bathing suit, and when the neighbor kids gawked at me, I felt naked and exposed. I became obsessed with the idea of a wall and began to gather roadside stones whenever I had access to Zoe's pickup. When I unloaded the truck, the neighbors watched, and the more they watched, the more stones I amassed.

In the meantime, I used a grommet kit to convert a nylon groundcloth into a shower curtain, which I hooked to a wire ring I hung from the straggly grape arbor overhead. With a length of hose, I showered privately behind the curtain— until the first wind. A cold wet cloth clapped against my skin. When I peeled myself free, I disassembled the rigging and bought a jumbo plastic basin. For the rest of my stay at the rental, I solar-heated jugs of water and then washed in my kitchen, unobserved, in the manner of Toulouse-Lautrec bathers.

In time the neighbors became less vigilant. I set aside my animosity and forgot about my wall. For amusement a villager from time to time asked me when I would build it and then warned me in earnest that my rock pile was an open invitation to snakes. Having made a spectacle of myself collecting stones, however, I postponed the embarrassment of carting them away.

One afternoon I entered my kitchen in time to glimpse a movement—the tail end of a snake scaling out of a Pheasant Brand Feta Cheese can, my potato bin. I froze. I knew it might be an adder—a deadly poisonous pug-nosed viper. I decided to follow its course while I determined a strategy, but it did not reappear. I crept up and peered down behind the tin, which sat on the floor against the wall. Instantly I saw the telltale snout. With lightning speed, I tipped the can slightly and slammed it down, pinning the snake underneath. Pressing urgently with one hand, I clenched a broom with the other and delivered a fatal blow.

Until that terrifying episode, I had felt alienated whenever the villagers shared their snake tales. My experience admitted me into their storytelling circle, but when I narrate my story, I refrain from mentioning the physical energy I expended and the personal embarrassment I risked in order to cast the treacherous drama played out in my kitchen.

When I returned home one day after the snake incident, my by then expendable rock pile had quietly disappeared.

men's work

'

When I moved to Elika in 1982 for an open-ended stay, I carried along kitchen articles, bedding, and hand tools to avoid having to purchase them in Greece. Once in Elika, however, I habituated whenever possible to local conditions and customs. Ironically, while I adjusted to the Turkish facility at my rental, most villagers had already piped water to featureless masonry cells built on their entry-level terraces to accommodate the "modern convenience." The more cosmopolitan villagers had even tiled the interiors from ceiling to floor and had installed rooftop solar water heaters that look like miniature spacecraft. Even as I schemed to restore a cottage window in my rental, a young man who had returned from a stint farming with relatives in New Jersey was installing Elika's first picture windows in his new house!

The wind had ripped severely weather-beaten shutters off the east window in my kitchen, and the frame had rotted and had to be replaced. I studied the existing design, measured, and calculated. Then I went to Neapolis, bought undressed wood from a lumber outfit, dragged it to another shop for planing, and transported it by bus to my job site.

With the assortment of tools I had brought from the States, the plastic-handled saw I had purchased locally, and wood on hand, I boldly knocked out the disintegrating frame. When I saw the gaping hole left in the wall, I gasped. How would I ever close it? I didn't have money to hire a craftsman, and if I had, I would not have known whom to ask or how to ask him. Necessity ruled. I gripped my saw and went out onto my second-story terrace turned workshop.

I started my framing late in the afternoon. My neighbor Sophia saw me as, with crochet work in hand, she stepped next door for coffee and a chat. She paused, observed the saw, and, before moving on, decried, "Men's work."

During the next few weeks, I undertook a host of other improvement projects at my rental. I whitewashed the interior. I stuffed rope insulation—from the States—around my windows. I replaced the original slate dry sink and drain hole with a stainless steel sink drained by plastic cut-and-glue plumbing. I built a footstool, an overhead hanging storage shelf, and a hinged sideboard in the kitchen.

One day I was trimming off the bottom of an interior door that no longer swung freely over the uneven floorboards. A man walking by noticed me with my saw once again in my hand. Uninvited, he climbed the stairs, pushed through the whiny gate, stepped to my side, and seized my tool. I knew the man to be a retired carpenter. Unintimidated, I reclaimed my saw from his hand before he transgressed further. "Can you?" he asked. "I can," I affirmed.

A two-seated bench sent me back to the lumber store in Neapolis. The proprietor is tall as a ship's mast and straight backed as a chair. His bay window, stern countenance, and gruff manner had always made him seem dispassionate. When I went in, I pantomimed my intent. He looked at me over his reading glasses, recognized me, and nodded approval. I climbed the ladder to the storage loft and searched through a stack of wood for a suitable plank.

While I was sighting down the edge of a board, another customer came in—a man. When he saw me in the loft, he turned to the proprietor with a doubtful expression. Facing his customer squarely, my friend simply replied, "She knows."

eggs, but no hens

I have not bought one single egg during all my days in Elika. Not because I don't eat eggs—I do. Not because I keep hens—I don't. But because the women in Elika give me eggs.

"Would you like some eggs?" A widow hailed me from her side yard where she had shooed chickens into her *kotetsi* (chicken coop) for the night. I had not seen her since Elika's original bakery closed a few years back, but when the bakery did operate, her house lay on my migration route. Having waved me to stop when she called out her offer, the woman hurried to the road to squeeze my arm before ducking into her house for the eggs. She sent me along with four.

"Shall I fry you some eggs?" my hostess asked. I had cleared my dishes of double-size servings of fish soup, salad, greens, and homemade bread. The weight in my stomach tricked my hearing; I disbelieved my ears and ignored the query. Before leaving the table, I praised the meal a final time, and my host unmistakably repeated his wife's question. He tore two squares of newspaper and individually wrapped two eggs for my breakfast as fast as I hastened to decline the well-intended offer.

"Come here," Rinoula called as I passed by. "I will give you some potatoes." "I just bought some," I reported as I entered her kitchen. She searched her mind for an alternative while her hands instinctively clutched a pair of eggs. She prepared them for transport in a plastic wrapper from a package of paper napkins and set them aside with a cucumber and a half-round of goat cheese. When I innocently asked what she had done that day, she showed me the *hilopita* covering every flat surface in the interior room including the bed. She bagged up some of the already dry pasta and added it to my bounty, along with a dish of dried tomato for sauce and a portion of freshly butchered goat meat—the components of a meal, in other words.

Greeks bestow gifts on strangers as an expression of hospitality and love. As long as I am a foreigner, the Greek housewife—the *nikokira*—will stuff the fruits of her labor into my *tagari*. If she has returned red-eyed from a day cutting onions, she lades me with onions. If she has painstakingly irrigated and harvested her summer garden, she packs me off with sweet tomatoes, baby zucchini, eggplant, and greens. When she has baked bread, I walk home munching the end pieces of a warm loaf. "Enough!" I cry. "Your house is not a supermarket." But my pleas for moderation go unheard, or at least unheeded. And as I stagger home, I marvel at the level of generosity and weight of effort the gifts represent.

The loaf of bread is baked from wheat flour, either store

bought or milled from the crop that has been planted, fertilized, reaped, and threshed. Equipment is required for baking: a kneading box, baking cloths, bread pans, and oven
implements. Then there is the domed outdoor oven,
branches to heat the oven, a donkey to deliver the branches,
and fodder to feed the donkey (or a pickup for transport
and gasoline to fuel it). Not to mention the wealth of experience required to regulate the oven temperature in spite of
fickle winds.

The *nikokira* learned her bread-baking skills and other
"women's work" from the women who raised her. Her re-
sponsibilities include all food preparation, clothes washing,
sewing, and sweeping, as well as whitewashing the house
inside and out and feeding the chickens. Some *nikokires* still
make yogurt and cheese, and a few continue to make soap.
Until recently, all sat at their looms long hours into the night
weaving homespun cottons, woolens, linens, and silks for
household use. And if they were luckless and bore daughters, they wove and decorated dowries for them. On top of
all this, the women share the field work equally with the men.

No wonder the hostess who offered to top off my
evening meal with a pair of fried eggs fell asleep the instant
she finished washing the dishes—by herself—and sat down.
No wonder the *nikokira* prefers drip-dry fabrics to natural
fibers, even though the electric iron eases the work. No wonder she covets automatic clothes-washing machines and
abandons her home ovens for inferior bakery bread.

I am not a *nikokira*. I dream about kneading dough for
my oven and roping branches onto my own packsaddle, but
I lead a cash-and-carry lifestyle. I buy bakery bread and proc-

essed cheese and hope for a slab of homemade cheese when I have a chunk of homemade bread to eat it with. I buy boxed detergent at Ksanthi's *bakaliko* and save my shrinking block of home-caked soap for only the toughest stains. And I accept the eggs the *nikokira* gives me with humility.

lament

"Matina! Matina!" I tried to project my voice across the narrow lane to my neighbor's house. "Matina," I pipped, and waited. At last—round, rosy, and smiling—Matina appeared behind the turquoise iron gate leading into her courtyard. "Please, Matina, would you bring me a *lemonita* from the *cafenio?*" The house I rented in Elika stood not more than two hundred meters from Ksanthi's *cafenio*, but I was too weary from illness to get there myself. Rather, I crawled back into bed, and shortly Matina—blue eyed—arrived with the drink. After I thanked her and assured her I could manage alone, she went back to her menu of activities.

At midday footsteps on my outside stairs announced Matina's return. She hooted, and I hailed back, and in she came balancing a large shallow bowl of egg–lemon soup she had carried all the way from her kitchen. After handing me the dish, she drew a chair to my bedside, seated herself, and began to speak. Preliminaries exchanged, she blew the dust off old sorrows stored in a long overlooked corner of her memory.

"I was the youngest of four children," she reported. "My mother died when I was two. The village ridiculed me even though I was an innocent child with no mother to defend me. This does not happen elsewhere," she observed, "but a village is a village, isn't it so?"

Heaving a sigh of resignation, Matina cast a glance at her hands crossed in her lap. I respected her silence, and then she accepted my presence as a flood of bitter truths spilled out. Her father had beaten her when she was young. Before he died, he disinherited her even though she had married without a dowry. She and her husband remain landless while thorns and branches overrun the family estate, now owned by two sisters in Athina and a brother in Canada. "My father didn't love me; I was orphaned twice," Matina lamented. "Life is an agony; I have suffered."

No doubt the neighbors have always known the facts Matina had confided in me, but not, it seems, the feelings. "Please don't tell the village," she beseeched me as she dried her eyes and turned to leave. "I let them think I'm happy."

flying the horizon

When I went to the Neapolis police headquarters to apply for my alien residency permit, I overheard an official in an inner office say, "Yes, she's the girl in Elika who is collecting olives." I had been working illegally for three weeks.

From the police offices I went to a store I had patronized only once before. The owner, remembering my face, associated me with rumors he had heard, and he announced to the other shoppers—all strangers to me—that I was the American who was living in Elika and gathering olives.

At least I was reputed to do good work, or so it seemed. Several days later, a man from Elika's satellite village, Ay Mammas, called upon Zoe. He knew she is my *koumbara*— "godmother," literally, but in this case the woman who looks out for me. He told her he had heard about me and that he wanted me to pick olives for him starting the next day, provided I was willing. Zoe relayed his message to me and added that he was my age and eligible. I wondered what stories our working relationship would generate and accepted his offer.

The next morning—a Sunday—I awoke on time and looked outside. By the dim light of dawn, I could see a skyful of clouds sagging like udders from the weight of their contents—on the verge of leaking. Surely it would rain sometime soon, somewhere nearby—maybe in Ay Mammas. Villagers stay close to their hearths when rain threatens. No need to submit to the cold and wet when work will wait. Why risk it, I asked myself.

Lambi is expecting me, I answered.

And I went.

When windfall olives are numerous enough to warrant the effort, olive gathering starts on the ground. When I arrived at Lambi's land, that's where I started. Lambi worked on the ground with me—there were just the two of us—and for a time, our curiosity about each other provided a diversion. He had greeted me with an apple he halved and shared, and he gave me a foil-wrapped orange-flavored sweet during a mid-morning break. He smiled often, more like a friend than a boss, and we glanced at each other frequently, though hesitating to catch each other's eyes.

When our eyes did meet, Lambi asked, "Will you stay in Greece? Will you marry here?"

I could see that Lambi farmed conscientiously. He had cultivated wheat—pricker free—in his olive grove. His trees were skillfully pruned. And at one point, when he combed olives from some branches, I could see how gently he approached his trees.

"If I am here during the next olive season, I would be glad to work for you again," I replied.

After a while my physical discomfort began to outweigh my curiosity about my employer. When my knees tired from squatting, I knelt on the ground—a ground saturated by predawn rainwater, rainwater that soaked into my pant legs. Wet pant legs, chilling my knees and making them stiffer. And stubborn fingers, stubborn because of the dank air. Other mornings when I had collected windfalls, my fingers balked until the sun came out. When it did, I competed with other pickers for patches of sunlight until the ambient temperatures rose. But this time the morning mist gave way to intermittent drizzle, and the dampness worked past my slicker, penetrated several layers of underclothing, and chilled me through.

On top of the chill, boredom. Boredom from picking innumerable slippery little round cold wet windfalls. Endless picking, like a hen's pecking. The monotony stretched the minutes, elongated the hours, five hours in all.

Finally at one o'clock Lambi's father Stratis arrived with lunch. He meant to stay warm; he was dressed in wool from head to foot. Trim stature, rosy complexion, bright blue eyes, and an easy smile. I could see where his son came by his wholesome good looks.

Lambi, his father, and I gathered under an olive tree, which deflected the rain. We sat on empty woven-plastic olive bags to keep our seats dry. And we ate: small pan-fried fish, greens, and fresh shredded cabbage dressed with dill, olive oil, and lemon juice. And homemade bread the widower Stratis had baked himself.

When we finished eating, Lambi offered to build an open fire to drive away my chill, but knowing that many Greeks still rested on the Lord's Day, I begged off the afternoon. Promising to return the next morning, I walked half a mile to the main road and caught a ride back to Elika.

After my second day working for Lambi, he did not invite me back. I don't recall what was said, but shortly I was to begin work for the Papadhakises anyway. I met Lambi and his father again later in the season when I returned to Ay Mammas for an outing.

On foot, I arrived in the center of Ay Mammas at midday and noticed Stratis mounting his horse. "Come and eat," he rang out. "Wonderful," I sang back. An inspiring presence on his horse, Stratis followed a steep rocky path uphill, in the opposite direction from the grove where we had met previously. Within easy walking distance—for me—we met Lambi and a number of hands. Stratis set out lunch for his son and me, and we ate. When we finished the meal, the others returned to the olive trees, and Stratis cleaned the blue-trimmed enamelware with a dandelion plant—yellow blooms and all.

When Stratis had packed up, he beckoned me farther uphill. I thought he intended to show me the footpath to a mountain chapel he had commented on earlier. Instead, he presented me with a white-plumed perspective of the sea, which shimmered like a mirror of the midnight sky.

I glided aloft while Stratis foraged edible wild greens— various species of dandelion. With a miniature hoe-like tool, he cut below the surface and extracted the tops whole. When his *tagari* was stuffed, I folded my wings, and we walked down the hill together.

Nearly a year later Stratis inquired about me from my *koumbaros*, Mihail, on behalf of his son Lambi. Mihail was right to discourage him. When I returned from my midday flight, I was no longer free.

mooring

When I collected olives for the Papadhakises, I synchronized my routine with theirs. I arrived at the storefront shortly before eight o'clock, and they arrived shortly after. Yiorgos presided over the ritual chair-mounting, and we paraded off to the trees—several hundred of them, their extensive root systems retaining acres of steep-sloped land just below Ay Mammas in a region called Nerantzia—"Bitter Orange."

On New Year's Eve morning, I arrived on schedule and the group appeared late. While I waited, my attention turned from the activity on the street around me to the sea that stretched toward a horizon obscured by haze. Mysteriously, a red glow in the southwestern sky toward the Mani silhouetted a distinctive funnel formation. It persisted long enough to provoke comments from the group as we proceeded to work, and then it disappeared.

When we reached the crest of the hill from which the Papadhakis field house first becomes visible, Yiannis announced that we would not be working that day—it would rain. The two-track road narrowed from there and plunged into a valley. After descending, we passed between two stately walnut trees, cut through a citrus grove, and crossed the seasonal stream we had been paralleling. Just as we began our ascent to the field house, a few snowflakes silently appeared, hung in the air for an instant, and vanished. We didn't turn back.

The moment we reached the field house, the weather changed abruptly; a wet Milky Way whirled around us. Everyone but Yiannis took refuge in the field house. Shortly he came in with an armful of fresh-cut olive boughs whitewashed with snow. He sectioned them and built a fire, which he ignited with the flame of a single match. Comfortable in a woolen hood and pigskin jacket, Yiannis went back out briefly and returned, this time with a burlap sack pregnant with oranges he had plucked from a nearby tree.

We women had pulled chairs to the hearth—I nested between Yiannis' wife Fani to my left and Yiorgos' wife Garifalia to my right. Our backs faced a corner iron bedstead, a small wooden table, and worn-out tools and outmoded gear hanging from nails and propped against the wall.

Garifalia's broad feet, clad in securely laced rugged leather shoes, were planted hip-width apart on the edge of the raised hearth. Her knees, too, were wide-spaced. Leaning into the fire, she rested her forearms on her thighs. Her powerful wrists relaxed; her bare hands fell over her knees.

Garifalia was still dressed for the cold in a pair of men's brown trousers, several sweaters, and, over all these, a black cotton flannel dress. Two layers of scarf, like swaddling clothes, wound around her head and across her chin. Everything about her was round, from the toes of her shoes to the crown of her head. And soft, the lifelines around her eyes and mouth as gentle as the folds in her flannel. And warm, her customary radiance glorified by the firelight that illuminated her.

Garifalia and I had been working together for several days, but we became acquainted by the fireside. She already knew that I am not married, but she learned that my mother and my father are both living and that I have one sister who has three children, all boys. I learned that she has three offspring—the oldest a daughter Athanasia who was beginning a career teaching kindergarten in Athina, the second a son Dhimitris who was studying veterinary medicine at the university in Thessaloniki, and the youngest a son Vangelis who was studying chemical engineering at Patras.

When the talk subsided and Garifalia had imbued me with her essence, I glanced out the small window behind her. I recognized the arched wooden top of a packsaddle. I knew it was sitting on the back of one of the donkeys who, like us, was waiting out the ground blizzard. The sight of the snow flying in the background made me shiver, so I refocused on the womb of warmth and serenity inside the field house.

The storm abated shortly, but left the round wooden rungs on the olive ladders too slippery to step on. So Garifalia removed her work trousers and dress and pulled on a skirt and lilac sweater. We left Yiannis and Fani behind and walked back to Elika through a dusting of snow bright like the fleece of the rambunctious kid goats that accompanied us.

When we arrived in Elika, Garifalia wanted to feed me, so after she stabled the goats, we settled in her kitchen. She laid a fire first and then set about preparing a hot meal for me: two fried eggs, pasta with *saltsa* and cheese, homemade bread, and a small glass of wine. After all that, two *koura-*

mbiedhes, though the Greeks usually end a meal with the fruit of the season rather than sweets. Garifalia washed my dishes with fire-heated water while I ate my sweets by the fireside. Then, preparing for lunch in the olive grove the next day, she stuffed cabbage into a pot on the hearth.

Garifalia would take her meal with her husband Yiorgos a little later—we had arrived back home before the *mesimeri*. But she had joined me at the table for a small plate of pasta and a taste of wine. Because we had already exchanged the essentials at the field house, we spoke very little in her kitchen—except to acknowledge the inviolable bond that had grown between us. "You are a good girl; I love you," she vowed. "I love you too," I promised.

telephone reception

I was to pick olives for the Papadhakises on Friday, so I left home at the appropriate hour and ambled toward the usual meeting place in front of the Papadhakis Brothers *bakaliko/ taverna*. Yiannis and Fani Papadhakis live above the family establishment. From a distance I watched Yiannis descend the exterior staircase, step onto the sidewalk, and enter the front door. His conspicuous Sunday attire reminded me that that day, January the seventh, was his name day. He would stay home from the olive grove to receive relatives, neighbors, and friends who would express their congratulations and sample the sweets Fani had dutifully baked for the occasion. (Yiannis did not bake sweets for his wife's name day on January the sixth.)

Farther down the street I saw Garifalia leading two donkeys. The donkeys must belong to Fani and Yiannis; today Garifalia and I will ride them, I speculated. I quickened my pace to join her at the storefront. She arrived ahead of me. Much to my dismay, she did not stop. She continued toward me, and when we met, she signaled me to follow. Reluctantly I turned on my heels and fell in behind her and our mounts. When we reached the same rock from which I had mounted Thea's Psari years before, we each climbed onto a donkey and rode out of the village toward Nerantzia.

Normally the chance to view a more distant horizon from a horse's or donkey's back delights me, but that morning I pouted all the way to the Papadhakis field house. When I had first glimpsed Garifalia with the donkeys, the idea that I would participate in the ritual chair-mounting danced in my imagination. When she walked past the storefront mounting site, all hope vanished.

No one was at fault. His brother's name day had not deterred Yiorgos from conveying and steadying the mounting chair for Garifalia and me. Rather, an open trench recently cut along the sidewalk prevented Yiorgos from crossing onto the street and cancelled the morning performance with my coveted role.

The trench, which ran past every shop and dwelling in Elika, would carry lines for private telephones. Prior to the arrival of these phones, Elika had only two such instruments. The first, a dull gray affair, arrived decades ago and is housed in a metal booth adjacent to the *cafenio* on Elika's *agora*. Villagers sit under a grape arbor outside the *cafenio* door and sip coffee or cola and chat while they wait to use the telephone. They take the risk that the line will be busy at the prearranged time to place or receive a call, or that the telephone will be dead because of brutal winds. All through their childhoods, when a call came in unexpectedly, the owner's children Soula and Yiannis searched the neighborhood for the person requested and ran messages to more distant residents.

One day I waited at the phone to call the carpenter in Neapolis to check the status of a window, a door, and frames he was making for the bathroom/storeroom addition I was building onto the house I had recently purchased. My neighbor's daughter was also waiting to place a call. When she saw me, she turned to a friend and explained that I was hauling materials, mixing mortar, and laying brick all by myself. "I'm crazy," I interjected. "Crazy not at all," she asserted. "Your semicircular wall looks beautiful on your curved terraced yard." The *cafenio* telephone connects Elika to the outside; by drawing telephone users together, it has also served as the local news switchboard.

A little girl owned Elika's second telephone. I don't know when or where she acquired it, but I saw it one day during the 1981 onion harvest. I was walking to the beach on the Marathia road when a group of onion cutters hailed me. They were resting in the shade of a roadside olive tree where they had lunched. When I approached them, three young girls clothed in sundresses giggled at me. They encircled a collection of toys that included two factory-made baby dolls and one bright orange plastic telephone with a white dial and handset. Today these girls probably go to high school in Sparti or Athina, where they undoubtedly call their parents on real telephones, and their parents probably answer on their own household sets.

The villagers welcomed the private phone. "It is the best gift that I could ever receive in my home," my friend Fofoula told me. "I don't care how much a telephone costs because I know it will give me relief and pleasure. I will be able to speak very often with my daughters in Athina, my son in Italy, and my relatives in America."

In recent years, many of Elika's children have gone to school, married, and settled in the metropolis, especially Athina. Soula and Yiannis are exceptions. She left school when she was sixteen, he is betrothed to a Neapolis girl, and both will probably settle in Elika. Like Fofoula, however, they are thrilled by the arrival of domestic phones because neither is any longer inclined to race through the village in search of the parents of increasingly numerous emigrant children who are calling home.

A few of us stubbornly continue to use the *cafenio* telephone. Some might think *I* dismiss the personal phone because the laying of cable spoiled a once-in-a-lifetime opportunity for me to take part in the Papadhakis street spectacular. Actually I simply prefer life in a household where the human voice is only heard live.

an unwelcome bedfellow

Death tolls rang at daybreak and woke me. "Who died?" I wanted to know. But I lay still as a corpse in my bed. I knew the slightest shift would draw icicles of air under my covers and displace the mantle of warmth my body had generated degree by degree during the night.

Wrapped in a turtleneck, a cotton flannel nightgown, and two pairs of woolen socks, I slept on a bedstead Zoe had furnished—a three-quarter-width iron bedstead I had sanded and painted midnight blue. Zoe's mother-in-law Yioryia had woven the accompanying indigo blue-and-white plaid cotton mattress stuffed with wool sheared locally. Winter after winter on this handsome mattress, Yioryia had slept warmly at her husband's side. Sleeping alone, I required an inordinate number of blankets to ward off the cold. Four I had brought from the States in the two footlockers that were trucked from Athina to Elika when I arrived. The fifth blanket made the critical difference. It was a dense handmade chocolate brown goat hair blanket Zoe had anticipated my needing.

Shrouded in bedcovers on this morning late in February, I grieved my circumstances. The olive season had drawn to a close. I did not miss working on wintry days; the sharp cold irritated me. I did not miss working on windy days; the sea of waving branches nauseated me. But I *missed* picking olives in hospitable weather, and I regretted not having a scheduled commitment to lure me out of bed in the morning.

I was not bereft of opportunities. At home there was my journal to update and always clothes to wash. Outside, I could accompany the villagers to their fields. Olive work is seasonal, but onions require a constant effort. I intended to acquaint myself with every facet of village life. But I lacked initiative; loneliness paralyzed me.

Zoe's absence and the language barrier accounted for my despair. Unable to articulate my feelings in Greek, I had depended on Zoe for intimate conversation. But she was called away early in the olive season. The longer her absence, the lonelier I became and the more isolated I felt in the company of my Greek-speaking co-workers. On mournful days, I wrestled my depression and hid my often tear-streaked face. Alone in the olive grove, I ached for home—not my vacuous, windswept rental home in Elika, but my well-insulated home in native America. But I knew that if I fled Elika in defeat, I would never return. And return I knew I must.

Zoe's absence outlived the olive season. To alleviate my loneliness, I retreated into books written in English. The author of *Tracks* inspired me; she had crossed the Australian desert alone with a surly camel.

The reading served its purpose, but to tear down the language barrier that alienated me from the village, I had to advance in Greek. I had been keeping a vocabulary book, and I studied Harris' *Colloquial Greek*. But these tools seemed impersonal, and the study itself felt isolating. To compensate, I wrote elementary journal entries in Greek and asked Ksanthi to correct them for me. She is my age and is one of a few women in Elika of her generation who completed high school. She took pride in tutoring me, and she enjoyed showing me off at the *cafenio* where I studied. "She reads and writes as well as speaks," Ksanthi announced to the afternoon cardplayers crowded around a table near the wood-burning stove.

I had banked on learning Greek from Greeks by interviewing villagers with the help of translators, but the translators appeared only sporadically. This not only frustrated my progress in learning Greek; it challenged my ultimate purpose—to shape village narratives into a portrait of Elika in transition. My anthropology teaching and editing experience had led me to my Elika project. Without completing it, how would I know where next to step? I had to remain on course, I concluded.

A clucking in the rafters punctuated the end of my dialogue. I looked up in time to watch a familiar gecko wriggle at lightning speed down a glacier-white wall. Envious of its resilience to the cold, I pulled on a knit cap and a pair of fingerless gloves as I reached for a book.

I read until shame, hunger, or the need to relieve myself—I forget which—forced me out of bed. A thermometer in the kitchen read forty-three degrees Fahrenheit, but I didn't light a fire because I was determined to go outside. I heated a pan of water on the stove, bathed, and quickly dried off with a face cloth. (Placing convenience above com-

fort, I had abandoned terry-cloth bath towels long before—
they are too bulky to hand wash.) After my invigorating
bath, I cooked Quaker oatmeal with cinnamon, raisins, and
fresh diced apple and ate it steaming hot with local honey
and Nou-Nou condensed milk.

Fortified, I donned an all-weather jacket and wet-
weather boots; then, without an agenda, I ventured into a
gloomy day. Instinctively, I went first to Ksanthi's *cafenio*. We
greeted each other, and I asked whether I had any mail.
None. "Who died?" I suddenly remembered to inquire.
Manolis, Thea's husband. His heart stopped mid-night, I
was informed.

Regret welled up within me. Manolis! I had never talked
with Manolis! I had lived in his house for weeks at a time,
and we had never become acquainted. He was reserved; my
language deficiency inhibited me. But my opportunity to
know him was now lost.

And Thea had lost a husband and companion. I wanted
to be with Thea. The lid of a coffin stood by her door. The
open casket occupied the center of the living room. I saw
Manolis' waxen face. Thea and I found each other and embraced. As we wept together, grief crashed against her like a
tidal wave. Another mourner pulled her from me and
helped her to a chair, but my friend's bewildered expression
drew me back to her side. As we held hands, Thea rocked
back and forth on her chair. She became agitated, rose,
wailed, and paced the length of the coffin before sitting
again beside me. Helpless before God, she crossed her arms
against her breast, groaned, and then bent forward and
buried her face in her hands.

Other mourners joined those of us already gathered

around the coffin. They told stories and sometimes laughed. I didn't know what to say, much less how to say it. I felt awkward and embarrassed. I had not thought to dress in black. I had not brought flowers to adorn the casket. I had not kissed Manolis' forehead or the ikon resting against his folded arms. I decided to leave. On my way out the door, Thea's cousin Matina grabbed me. She pulled me into the kitchen and sat me down for a bowl of goat soup. The immediate family was eating in an adjacent room. None of the other mourners were being fed. How could Matina think of the American girl at a time like this, I wondered.

Finally I left Manolis' wake and went home to my rental. At dusk the church bells rang. Respectful villagers emerged from their houses, joined the funeral procession, and followed Manolis to the cemetery where he was laid to rest inside a ring of cypress trees. Despondent, I stayed home by my hearth; I knew Thea and Manolis would excuse me.

After dark I cooked a light supper and then read by the fireside. The wind came up. Window shutters flapped on rusty hinges. The velocity increased. The lights flickered. Blasting through open windows in the lower-level storeroom, the wind rushed through the spaces between the sagging floorboards and lifted the center of one of Zoe's woolen rag rugs off the floor. The sight of the rug momentarily suspended in the air made me shiver. Which is worse, I asked, moving from a warm bed into a cold room in the morning, or moving from a warm fire into a cold bed at night?

I smothered the fire. The cold is an unwelcome bedfellow, I grumbled. Thea has plenty of warm blankets, I reassured myself as I drew the bedcovers around me.

martha

I was looking for Martha, and I knew I was within range. But I found no evidence of her—until my ears caught the sound of an ill-tempered voice riding past me on a downhill wind. I retraced its course with my eyes, and there she was, a black speck as yet indistinguishable from other black specks—a dark-clad goatherd among dark-coated goats.

Certain that Martha had spotted me before I spotted her, I waved hello and turned off the two-track mountain road I had been walking. I picked my way around spiny thicket and rock outcrop as I headed toward her. When I drew close enough to hear the familiar tinkle of goat bells, I began to shout introductions into the wind. First I answered the question every Greek asks any stranger: where are you from? "I am an American, but I live in Elika. Have you heard about me?" She showed no sign of recognition, so I barraged her with information about myself. "I went to school with Zoe's cousin in America. I was a teacher for fifteen years. I have lived in Elika for over a year. I rent a house near Ksanthi's *cafenio*. I pick olives and take photographs. . . ."

Breathless from talking while climbing uphill, I paused when I arrived at the base of the terrace wall where Martha waited for me. An arm's length away, I reached up to shake her hand. She stepped to the edge of the terrace, reached down, clasped my hand *and* my forearm, and—taking me entirely by surprise—yanked me, scrambling for a foothold, up the stone face of the meter-high wall.

I was stunned by the burst of human energy that whisked me onto the terrace above, because a Greek is not likely to expend energy unnecessarily. I had learned this from Yiannis Papadhakis when I picked olives for him the previous winter. "You do good work, but you tire yourself scaling terrace walls. You should save yourself and walk around." Heeding his words, when I reached for Martha's hand, I had already plotted my course around the terrace wall.

When I stood toe to toe with Martha and sized her up, the means of my delivery awed me even more. I *am* lean, but I am considerably taller than she. And if not so very old, she seemed so much used, like a timeworn chair one tests before trusting. To this day I ask myself what irrepressible need or instinct compelled this woman to bare her strength thus to me and to God rather than to point a way around the wall. Set off by her tanned and wrinkled complexion, Martha's sky blue eyes spoke the answer: they danced with light like the glistening afternoon sea far below.

"*Mouskema,*" Martha said as she lifted her hand off my sweat-soaked shirt and hobbled off. Before I could intervene, she had selected and single-handedly hefted a sizeable rock to the downwind side of a natural carob windbreak growing nearby. "Sit here," she ordered, "so you won't take cold." Slipping into a warm sweater I had carried in my day pack, I minded her and sat down.

Martha, of course, had dressed for an uninterrupted day in an unusually cool and unrelenting October wind. A black head scarf was secured by a knot that she retied as we became acquainted. Her dark, nubby, three-quarter-length coat—fastened with a large safety pin—nearly concealed a blue print cotton flannel dress layered over a heavy sweater. Her rough black woolen skirt was lengthened with a band of mismatched fabric. A thin, tattered, dark red apron completed her wardrobe. Oh, and cut-down ill-fitting rubber boots pulled over socks—a black pair underneath a tan pair. The holes and ravels in the outer ones proclaimed her profession . . .

. . . From which I had distracted her. Suddenly, like a mother who senses an absent child's mischief, Martha flashed back to her goats, which had scattered. Having forgotten her anger while we laughed together, the cantankerous Martha now resurfaced; instantly she began to regale her wayward charges with the curses and rebukes that had signaled her location to me earlier. And as she trudged after them, stiff-legged, over rough terrain, she picked up loose stones and hurled them overhand with such a vengeance that they missed their targets widely and bounced off the ground no more than a few steps in front of her.

Torn between the demands of her capricious flock and the temptation of my company, Martha returned after reforming the herd. I found the pomegranate I had brought and gave it to her. Receiving it she vowed, "I shall keep it as a souvenir. I shall remember you until I die." Before I left, she disappeared long enough to grab two tree-ripened figs. She peeled them before she set them in my hands.

what became of the pomegranate

A blank facade with a pair of widely spaced windows upstairs. A centered double door below. Ksanthi's *bakaliko* sits off the road and gapes at the backs of the houses to each side. In contrast to a freshly whitewashed stucco, the brown-colored trim has been allowed to dull through lack of interest—something like the dusty coat of the donkey tethered by the door.

I had chauffeured Kyriakos earlier, and now I went into the *bakaliko* to buy some cleaning supplies for the house I had rented from his wife. A man inside, presumably the owner of the donkey, danced Zorba-like when he saw me. He quieted only after purchasing and giving me a cellophane-wrapped packet of double-chocolate sandwich cookies. His intent to celebrate our meeting was clear, but his gift bewildered me all the same! I had never before noticed, much less eaten, factory-baked sweets in Elika. And although the man looked familiar, I could not place him (or his donkey) with certainty. I thanked him truly and left still feeling puzzled.

That fall, memories of an earlier hike to Siamenes, a mountain valley high above Elika, drew me back. In one place, the roots of ancient olive trees pushed silently toward a source of water undisclosed beneath a dense clutter of surface stone. Nearby, almost hidden by a thicket of pink-flowered oleander, a spring of liquid crystal gurgled forth. Two reliable geographic features—touchstones for a solo traveler.

At Siamenes I also hoped to encounter Andonis, the man I had met there the previous year. He had left the farming to his heirs when he took up goatherding twenty-odd years before. As I approached the landmark oleander off to my right, I heard bells jingling to my left. I looked in time to see how Andonis, who was approaching me, negotiated a particularly steep decline. He established a footing against the base of an olive tree, clinched the trunk with his arm, and completed his descent without slipping. A match for his nimble goats, I could see.

As we gripped each other's hands, Andonis' jubilant greeting tipped me off. He was the man at Ksanthi's *bakaliko*. As we connected this time, I recalled our first encounter in Siamenes. Andonis had walked me to his side-by-side double *kalivi* (hut), a make-do masterpiece a stone's throw away. We went into a single room just large enough to accommodate a bed, a cookstove, and a trunk. He unlocked the trunk, withdrew a jar of cherry sweet, and spooned a serving onto a china saucer for me. When I had eaten, he offered me a companion glass of water—a tradition no more dispensable because Andonis lived so far outside Elika, but water all the more precious because he had hauled it from there by donkey.

While Andonis prepared my sweet, I occupied myself matching evidence to the rumors I had heard about him and his second "wife" Martha. Andonis' room clearly afforded only enough space for one, and it leaned back-to-back against a second room, equally small and accessible only by its own exterior door. I supposed that Martha had equipped that room with her own bed and cookstove, just as I had heard. Since Martha was nowhere to be seen, I speculated that she was out tending her own separate flock.

Meeting me in Siamenes this second time, Andonis kept one eye on his goats while we spoke long enough to re-affirm our friendship. Then he gave me his door key and pressed me to help myself to a Turkish delight (a candy) and water. I went to his *kalivi*, not to consume his provisions, but to sit for a spell and imagine how Andonis might experience his living quarters. Then, leaving his key where he had told me, I moved on.

I had felt close to Martha when I sat against the wall she and Andonis shared. When I left the *kalivi*, I experienced an irrepressible urge to meet her, and I hiked farther up the valley to find her. When I did, I was surprised she had not heard about me. Her cohort had recalled me so vividly after our first meeting in Siamenes that he bought me cookies at Ksanthi's. I knew my reputation had spread as far as Neapolis by then. Had Andonis not bothered to tell Martha about me? If Andonis and Martha shared neither bed nor cook-stove, a flock, nor gossip about strangers, what, besides a wall, did they share?

The last time I saw Andonis was exactly four years after we first met. He was sitting by the roadside near the spring in Siamenes when I found him. Why was he sitting? Where was his flock? He greeted me warmly and commented on how long it had been—nearly a year—since I had visited him. But his lackluster tone spelled trouble. He told me he had been ill over the winter and that his flock had been sold while he recuperated in the village. He missed his goats. After our conversation, Andonis paced, downhearted, back to Elika. Nothing at the *kalivi* seduced him to stay—no flock to husband come morning, and Martha was gone.

Two years earlier, an eye injury had necessitated Martha's hospitalization. Her flock was sold while she convalesced at her brother's house in Finiki, another village in Lakonia where she had married and raised a family before joining Andonis in Siamenes. Recovered, she stayed in Finiki.

As Andonis drifted to Elika, I followed the road up past the lonely double *kalivi*. Goats were nowhere to be seen, but I could almost make out bells resounding in the wind.

A year later, I passed by Andonis' Elika resort on my way to Siamenes. His son, who lived next door, informed me: Andonis had died during the winter. I proceeded to Siamenes and the desolate double *kalivi*. The question recurred: what had Andonis and Martha shared? Perhaps an undeniable passion for this exalted mountain realm—the same passion that draws me back time and again.

■

Not long after her departure, I traveled to Finiki to visit Martha. I had met her only twice in Siamenes, but I wanted her to know I remembered her. In the village, I was lucky to find a man who knew the way up a repeatedly forking unpaved road through breathtaking country to her remote summer grazing land. He took me there in his van. When we arrived and I stepped down from the vehicle, I called to signal my approach. Martha shouted back. When I reached her and she recognized me, she was mystified. "How did you know where to find me? How did you ask for me?"

Martha lives during the dry months in a three-sided *kalivi* large enough for a cot and a cook pot set over an earthen hearth—no more. When I arrived, she was heating the morning milk. She skimmed off the curd and passed me a serving. Later I gave her the melon I had taken her, and I had to ask whether she remembered what I had given her in Siamenes. "An apple?" she ventured. "No, a pomegranate," I reminded her. "Yes," she reflected, "I remember now. That evening when I saw Andonis, I said, 'See what the girl brought.' I shared it with him."

a beacon in the night

"It's a *mantri!* It's a *mantri!*" Lambi Houlis brayed. "I corralled my sheep there. It's stood roofless for decades," he bellowed.

It was June the twenty-sixth, 1984, a momentous day for me, the day I officially purchased my house in Elika. I had agreed to pay Lambi two hundred fifty thousand drachmas or slightly over two thousand United States dollars for an orphaned, aged, peasant house, a few square meters of neglected land, and two pathetic olive trees. (The sale of my forsaken Pinto wagon two years earlier provided me with almost the entire purchase price.)

That morning in a records office in Monemvasia, Lambi and I had both signed the deed in ten different places. (Greek custom required me to sign as Thordis Robert Simonsen—Robert is my father's first name—because I was unmarried.) Mihail Tsigounis, Elika's priest Papa Nikolas (there on church business), and the official's wife all witnessed the signing and the transfer of money. Then Mihail drove Lambi and me to the tax office in the nearby town Molaoi, where the purchase tax would be assessed.

On the way to Molaoi, Mihail instructed Lambi to report a purchase price of seventy thousand drachmas so that I would be charged a lower tax than one based on the actual sale price. At first Lambi took offense; he thought Mihail was accusing him of charging too much for the house. But Lambi caught on, and when the time came, he reported the lower amount. When the value was challenged, he, like the proverbial mule, refused to budge.

In spite of Lambi's obstinance, I was presented with what seemed like an exorbitant tax for a roofless house assessed, sight unseen, at very close to the actual purchase price. Fortunately, Lambi agreed to pay half the tax. Then, to consummate our exchange, he bought Mihail and me a sweet at a confectioner's shop on Molaoi's *agora*.

On the way back to Elika, I asked Lambi what he would do with the income from the sale of the house. He said he would pay rent on his daughter's apartment in Thessaloniki where she was taking a degree in physical education. The conversation shifted from spending to earning when Lambi moaned that the house sale proceeds had eaten two valuable days of the onion harvest. Pulling and bagging onions is physically exhausting work. Lambi, who was white-headed but youthful and burly at age fifty-eight, nevertheless complained, "My hands hurt, my feet hurt, my back hurts. . . ." His effort; his children's ease.

I had begun laying brick at my house three weeks prior to the purchase, and each day I too had experienced physical discomfort. Rather than diminish the effect of Lambi's lament, however, I kept my admission to myself.

When we arrived back in Elika, I bought Lambi an ouzo

at his neighborhood *cafenio*—the telephone *cafenio*—in order to acknowledge publicly my satisfaction with my purchase. I think Lambi and I each believed we had profited more than the other from the transaction. He had sold a property useful only for penning sheep. I had bought a priceless view of Elika and the Lakonian Gulf.

I had anticipated a lifelong association with Elika ever since my homecoming in 1982, and I yearned increasingly for a house of my own. I had searched tirelessly for the suitable dwelling, but rejected one possibility after another. I dismissed one house because the neighboring houses were too close, another because I was unwilling to negotiate with six owners, another because I would have had to carry all my water by bucket up a steep narrow trail, another because it was structurally unsound. I cannot say what possessed me to turn around and buy a roofless ruin set fifty meters downhill from the closest road. When I weighed the pros against the cons, the cons—panoramic view notwithstanding—far outweighed the pros. During restoration, every brick, bag of cement, truckload of sand, roof tile, floorboard, plumbing fixture, and window sash would have to be transported down a multi-terraced slope. And during residency, every melon and cooking gas bottle would have to be carried down the same steep decline. Impractical? Unthinkable!

And the house! It would require a septic well, a bathroom and storeroom, additional window openings, new window and door lintels, additional chimney and wall height, a restored fireplace and wall niches, floors, water lines, electricity, all-around tuck pointing inside and out, and a reinforced-concrete top ring—not to mention the new roof.

In spite of all the drawbacks, after I discovered the house I went straight to its owner to find out whether it was for sale. Lambi promised to consider the possibility.

By the time I left Lambi's house, night had fallen. On my way back to my rental, I witnessed one of Greece's innumerable shooting stars. It blazed across heaven with remarkable speed and light—a soul that, having been lost, travels the path home. I took the star into account and decided to purchase Lambi Houlis' house at any price.

kotetsi song

My landlady's relatives cultivated the field between my rental and the outhouse. Some seasons I skirted a crowd of ripe tomatoes; others, an audience of red onions. Just beyond that field, another family planted a patch of peanuts. One day the words of a love song drifted through my window, and I looked out. The husband and wife, both sitting on their haunches, were pulling up peanuts and bagging them. The music streamed out of a battery-powered radio nested at hand, barely visible among clods of earth. Determined not to be an agent of technological change when I moved to Elika, I had left my portable cassette player in the States, but hearing the Greek song made me wish for the companionship of music from home.

Shortly thereafter, Vaso, Mihail's cousin's wife, gave me a sack of eggs and tomatoes to take home and then invited me to join her family for dinner. Her husband, three teenagers, and I seated ourselves around an adequately sized table in a dining room so small it barely accommodated six chairs. Vaso's chair remained empty throughout the meal; she busied herself serving the rest of us. We ate fried eggs and potatoes topped with a meat *saltsa*, fried eggplant and zucchini, village salad with feta cheese, and homemade bread—with apricots following. All the while the other guest—a colossal, remote-control TV set—blared in my ears and fizzled.

In my adventures around the village, I also began to notice sophisticated component stereo equipment purchased duty-free by merchant marines. And when I walked up to Rinoula's husband Nikos to photograph him tying bundles of wheat with his hand-braided wheat ropes and he advised, "You need video," I knew—without a doubt—that I wouldn't plant new ideas in any villagers' heads if I brought my cassette player to Elika. The next time I returned from the States, the tape player came with me. And cassettes—everything from Joan Baez, Bob Marley and the Wailers, and Alexandre Lagoya to Ludwig van Beethoven.

I also brought along the two thousand dollars I had acquired from the sale of my car. With that sum I paid for the house I had arranged to purchase prior to my trip home. Even before the deed to the house had been transferred officially, I began to add on a storeroom and a bathroom.

After several weeks, for different reasons, two neighbor women—Sophia and Vasiliki—asked to visit my house in Maravelianika, a neighborhood a few minutes' walk up the hill from my rental. Sophia, the skeptic, wanted to see the results of a woman's construction efforts. Vasiliki, the romantic, wanted to see the embodiment of my dream, the dream of a simple stone dwelling, a dream we shared.

We agreed they should visit my house together one day at dusk. Spiffed up in Sunday dresses and shoes and bearing gifts of ouzo and a Greek rose liquor, they arrived at my roofless, doorless, floorless, obviously uninhabitable shell. As we toured the site, Sophia responded blandly while Vasiliki rejoiced at the stonework and arched windows and observed, "You love your house. It's like a church."

Two days later, after dark, Vasiliki arrived at my rental door with some tomatoes. I welcomed her inside. I had been eating a late supper in the company of Beethoven. Not knowing how familiar or appealing the sound, I asked her, "Do you like it?" "I listen to your music from my porch," she replied. "Can't you play it more loudly?" When the Third Symphony ended, I played the Sixth—the *Pastorale*—and Vasiliki and I basked wordlessly in its mellifluence.

One afternoon after that I saw Sophia crocheting alone in the shade of the mulberry tree in her courtyard, and I joined her. "Why do you play your music so loudly?" she asked as she stood up and turned toward her entry stairs. She went inside and reappeared shortly with a small serving tray. As she descended the stairs, she sang a little song:

> Her house is a *kalivi*;
> Her house is a *mantri*;
> Her house is a *kotetsi*.

Accepting the *kourambiedhes* and water she offered me, I intoned:

> My house *is* a *kalivi* (hut);
> My house *is* a *mantri* (sheep corral);
> But my house is *not* a *kotetsi* (chicken coop)!

"I didn't know you could understand," she explained sheepishly.

karekla

Once every week or two, I shop in Neapolis for provisions—food, building supplies, and postage stamps. Loaded down with purchases, I return to Elika on the bus. In July and August, like bees hiving at dusk, Greek children and grandchildren from Athina and abroad descend on their ancestral towns and villages all over Greece and complicate the boarding process.

One summer day I was standing with an older man from Elika at the head of a crowd waiting for the bus in Neapolis. When the vehicle pulled up, I sensed a familiar wave of excitement pass through the group. Choosing to observe rather than to participate in the impending stampede, I cut myself out of the herd. My companion held his leading position. When the doors opened, he raised and locked his elbows—like horns—and charged onto the cattle car where he claimed a front seat. Finally I boarded. The man from Elika muttered an unfamiliar word and waved me into the adjoining seat he had somehow saved for me.

This phenomenon occurred at one of those times when I

was more committed than usual to extending my Greek vocabulary, and I wanted to know what the man had said. When I got home, I searched my dictionary for a word that fit the context of the boarding experience and began with "*zou*"—the only syllable I absolutely remembered. The first word that caught my eye was *zoulisma*, meaning "squeezing, crushing." The meaning fit, but the word was too long. Looking again, I found the word *zougkla*, "jungle." The length was right, but the sound did not ring true. Perusing further, I found *zourla*, "lunacy." Exactly!

I am a visual learner, and because I saw the word *zourla* in print, I remember it. But I do not have a facility for foreign language, so I may hear a word repeatedly without mastering it. The word *kotetsi* defied my memory, even though every household has a chicken coop, and the word is commonplace. No wonder I was more pleased than offended when I understood my neighbor Sophia's "*Kotetsi* Song."

When I first arrived in Elika, all I could say was *dhen katalaveno*, "I don't understand." Soula, the daughter of the owner of the telephone *cafenio*, was then an impish five-year-old. Having befriended me, she stayed underfoot—like an unweaned kid goat—and prattled incessantly. Frustrated by my inability to understand, I spoke my phrase to her. I reasoned that the message, spoken in Greek, negated its meaning; Little Soula never stopped chattering.

Mastering one word at a time, I gradually acquired a large enough vocabulary to leave my dictionary at home. At first I celebrated my arrival at this level of proficiency, but I have discovered a pitfall. Instead of learning new words, I tend now to be more creative with my existing vocabulary.

When I hear myself say, "a souvenir in my mind" because I do not know the Greek word for "memory," I feel a little ashamed.

The villagers constantly remind me that Greek is a difficult language. They are patient and forgiving. "I don't know enough words," I insist. "You know how to say everything," they retort. To prove his point, one villager pushed his chair away from the dinner table, squatted on the floor, clucked, made his hand out to be a nest, and in it laid an imaginary egg, which he presented to me. "This is how Greeks ask for eggs in America," he teased. "You don't do this." His dramatic rebuttal closed the case—for the moment.

Every time I visited my *yiayia* Irini, from the first time we met until she took to her deathbed, she impressed upon me the importance of learning the language, and she instructed me. Wrapping her fingers around the slat of a chair back, she pronounced *ka re kla*. Then slapping her hand on a table top, *tra pe zi*. And clinking a spoon against a glass, *po ti ri*. When the lesson ended, she tapped her staff resolutely on the floor, and laughed. Then she scooted her chair next to mine and silently rested a hand on my knee.

long days' journey into the night

Because I learn Greek one word at a time, I often recall the particular person who spoke a new word to me and the exact situation that called for it. One evening I met my rental neighbor Stavros on the street outside the telephone *cafenio*. He was on his way into the *cafenio* to collect his newspaper, which arrives daily by bus from Athina. I had just left my personal news reporter and commentator, Zoe—she lives across the street from the same *cafenio*.

"*Tha ta kataferis? Tha ta kataferis?*" Stavros asked affably. I looked puzzled, so he pointed in the general direction of my house, where I was building the addition, and said, "Your house, much work." Perhaps his wife Vasiliki had reported my bricklaying to him the evening she visited my house with the more critical Sophia. Or perhaps Stavros himself had seen the American girl laying brick. My house sits on a tiny promontory beside a ravine that separates my lone dwelling from the village to the west. At work, I am visible from several points in the village.

"Much work, I know!" I conceded. Then, like any Greek

confronting the inevitable, I shrugged, "What can I do."

When I reached my rental, Stavros' first words echoed in my head, so I looked up the meaning in my dictionary. *Katafero*—"to accomplish." Stavros had asked, "Can you accomplish it?" I don't think I had ever asked myself *whether* I could; I simply knew I wanted to and would.

Stavros' question reminded me of the Greek attitude toward do-it-yourself work. The attitude is captured by an old saying Mihail had told me when he tried to discourage me from buying a *mantri*. "The vineyard requires a vine grower; the beehive requires a beekeeper; the ship requires a sailor." Taking Mihail's side, his mother had chimed in with a local expression that conveyed, tongue in cheek, the same message: If all the bees make honey, joy for my uncle Leftheri! (Leftheri was a beekeeper.) I knew the village would ridicule me for failing a specialist's job, not for trying. "Can you accomplish it?" the question reverberated.

Well, when I was young, my mother always told me I could do anything, I reasoned. Tools and construction have always appealed to me. Drawn by curiosity, I always stuck by my father whenever he built or fixed things at home. When a house was under construction in the neighborhood, I used to explore it after hours, and I built a soapbox jalopy and tree house with my playmates.

I've always been handy. Before I moved to Greece, I laid a three-course brick retaining wall around my vegetable garden. And at my rental in Elika I had already single-handedly accomplished an array of improvement projects. To equip me for my house restoration, I brought a book on masonry techniques from the States, and before leaving for Greece I consulted with a concrete contractor. "Can you accomplish it?" Stavros had asked. I learned Greek one word at a time. I will build my addition one brick at a time, I resolved.

I prepared for construction by finding the center of my five-meter-wide, south-facing exterior wall with a tape measure. I set a stake in the ground at the midpoint and tied a string to the stake. Two hundred thirty centimeters out, I tied a pointed stick to the line and, using the apparatus like a compass, I scribed an arc on the ground from one end of the wall to the other. I cleared the weeds from the semicircular area I had marked, and along the arc line I dug a trench to bedrock with my mattock. I mixed concrete and poured it into the trench; then I dug a second trench that halved the semicircle and poured concrete into it.

Having poured the footers for the walls of my addition, I ordered two exterior doors with frames and one window and frame from Neapolis—I would set the frames in place and build my walls around them. Then I hired the local trucker—the critical Sophia's husband—to deliver a load of bricks from Neapolis. I accompanied him to the brickyard and back. After he dumped the bricks at the roadside, I groaned, "I have to carry every brick to my house. It's not work for a woman." "No," he disagreed, "it doesn't matter that you are a woman; the pay is the same. You carry bricks; I carry bricks; the pay is the same. Besides," he confided as he gazed at my house, "you have taste."

Sanctioned to do "men's work" by a man too tradition-bound ever to undertake "women's work," I began to build my walls. Every evening, about the time the last shrill-pitched cicada finally stilled, I carried bricks, sand, and water to my house. In spite of the late hour, I sweated like a dray horse in harness. But the view of the sea, yawning at sunset, blinded me from the strain.

Every day under a blazing hot sun, I laid brick. When my neighbors Eleni and Andonis returned at midday from their Marathia garden via the trail running alongside my house, they reprimanded me for working in the open through the heat of the day. And when my mentor Irini learned that I worked on Sundays, she waved her staff threateningly in my direction.

Riding against the tide of Elika's apprehensions, I held my course. Brick by brick I laid each row, and row by row my walls rose. Before long, Eleni and Andonis were calling out as they passed, "Hello, Master, how goes the work?"

By July the Fourth, my walls were shoulder high. I was working awkwardly from an inadequate extension ladder when Lambi, en route to his nearby orange grove, walked up and evaluated my progress. "Master craftsman!" he beamed. "I don't know how to do these things," he granted. "How did you learn?"

Gratified by Lambi's acknowledgment, I worked on with renewed heart. A few days later, I encountered a woman in the village. "Jealous masters will report you to the police for working without employment papers," she bantered. Could I take her to mean that the women of Elika might forgive me for breaking with tradition?

Three weeks later, Lambi reappeared at my house with a delivery of cement. "What a beautiful thing I see," he rejoiced. "When you finish your house, you should build bread ovens," he boasted. (Only the most highly skilled masons build the dome-roofed bread ovens.) "I will tell them at the *cafenio* that you are the finest craftsman."

The sun got hotter. The cicadas screeched more loudly.

My body ached for rest. But I worked on. Eventually I improvised forms and poured curved reinforced concrete lintels over my window and doors. Finally, close to my prescheduled departure date, I laid the uppermost course of bricks.

The next day, I stopped at Pepi's *cafenio* for refreshment, and I met his brother Nikos, my neighbor the shepherd from whose *mantri* I had toted water all summer. Seeing me, another villager asked Nikos whether my construction work was as beautiful as he had heard. "My Virgin Mary!" he swore. The glint in his eyes told the rest of the story. Turning to me, he asked why I wasn't working on such a cool day. "Instead you work on the hot days," he chided. He had passed my house many times and knew my work habits well. "I'm not working because I've finished building my walls. Can you believe it?" I asked. "I believe it," he said. "You have patience and persistence."

The day before I left, I paid Irini my farewell visit. I reported my summer's progress. She tapped approval with her staff and foresaw the day the village would dance on the wheat-threshing circle adjacent to my house to celebrate its completion.

Lastly, on the eve of my departure, I went to the telephone *cafenio*, Lambi's *cafenio*, to say goodbye to Little Soula. "Come here," my rental neighbor Stavros called. Putting down his newspaper, he stood up and reached to shake my hand. "You accomplished it! You accomplished it well!" he announced. Lambi had kept his word, I marveled. "I worked too slowly," I apologized out loud. Stavros disagreed. "To travel far, one must travel slowly."

the kids get my goat

"Wait your turn!" I scolded. "I'll come back for you," I promised. And I efficiently maneuvered a fifty-kilo sack of Portland cement into my carry-all washtub and dragged it from the road to my house. There I dumped the bag alongside several others I had already transported in like manner that morning.

I buy my cement from Lambi Houlis who sells it, as well as sacks for bagging olives and onions, from a storeroom on the main street under his mother-in-law Thea's residence. He always delivers my cement because I don't have transportation of my own, and he seems to like helping me transform the *mantri* I bought from him. In the past Lambi packed the cement on his horse, two bags at a time, to my work site. When he pulled the ropes to release the paper bags, they usually thudded to the ground without breaking.

Since 1986 Lambi has delivered my cement in his chartreuse Nissan pickup. He leaves the sacks at the roadside, and I transport them to my house. Initially I moved the cement—as well as plastic bags of hydrated *asvesti* (a lime source) and loose sand and gravel—in my plastic washtub. I secured a rope to one end and dragged it behind me. The washtub glided downhill easily because it was slippery, and it was easy to pull back uphill because it was lightweight. When the first corner wore through, however, it leaked sand, and I had to dispose of it. Seeing that the house restoration would consume numerous washtubs, and being too ecologically minded to keep throwing away nonbiodegradable worn-out ones, I went to a carpenter in Neapolis who replicated the washtub in wood. I assembled the pieces he obligingly cut to fit, and I attached hardwood runners to the bottom so the box would slide without wearing.

This single carry-all has cycled from road to house to road hundreds of times. One day I promised an impatient passenger a ride. After I dumped my last bag of cement, I paused long enough to blot trickles of sweat from my brow with the sleeve of my blue cotton chambray work shirt and trudged back uphill. "Your turn," I told my passenger, a six-month-old white male kid goat. He hopped into the sled, and I gave him a ride to my house. His snow-white sister skipped alongside.

The kids belonged to a she-goat usually tethered near a mulberry tree at an abandoned old house just down from the road and east of my path. Unlike other kids their age, these were not hobbled. Over time, they became increasingly brazen. When I kept my promise and gave the male kid a ride, I bought a sledful of trouble.

My playfulness apparently appealed to the kids who, after the ride, preferred my company to their mother's. I enjoyed their spirit until they began to follow me into the bathroom where I was laying a floor with fieldstones I had collected one at a time from nearby fields and roadsides. My bathroom simply was not large enough to accommodate me, my sand buckets and mortar box, stones, guidelines, and two nosy kids. When they first ventured in, I casually flapped my hands and said "Git." Respectfully they scampered out, but no sooner had I turned my back than they impudently charged back inside. Yelling, clapping my hands, and stomping my feet, I tried to let them know I meant business. They looked at me mockingly and danced on my neatly tooled wet grout. Irked by their defiance, I dashed a pailful of water on them. They bolted out of range, then warily returned. Exasperated, I beat feverishly on the empty water pail, but the novelty of my behavior outweighed the discomfort I inflicted, and they stuck by me.

Their audacity infuriated me, and the game turned into a contest I was determined to win. Forgetting my aversion to corporal punishment, I cut a switch from one of my still, silent olive trees and desperately chased my antagonists, who sped just out of reach ahead of me. Fortunately, before it was too late, I recognized the likelihood of falling on my face and hurting myself instead of the kids, and I quit the chase. Embarrassed, but uninjured, I caught my breath. When I gathered my wits, I hit upon a more graceful solution to my problem.

That evening when the owner came to feed and water her livestock, I informed her that the footloose kids were interfering with my work. "Beautiful," she replied, and went about her chores. Often this woman does not hear at all, and when she does hear, she integrates what she takes in into a reality uniquely her own. I went away feeling helpless, defeated.

The next morning, shortly after I arrived at my house to work, the woman appeared, untied her she-goat, and led it and the kids away. "She did understand!" I rejoiced. Later I learned that my complaint had nothing to do with her action. Rather, the time simply had come for her to move to a bungalow at Marathia for the summer, and of course her goats went with her.

If only I had trusted that the disruption would be short-lived, I reflected, I wouldn't have let the kids get my goat.

field day

The glass and metal door of my rental house clattered against its frame. "Thordis! Thordis!" a woman's voice cried. I swung the door open wide. "Can you cut onions tomorrow?" Krisoula appealed. She was the third villager to approach me that day. "No," I replied, "I must be at my house; the plumber is coming from Neapolis. I'm sorry." "All right, Thordis," she said. As she turned to leave, it struck me that Greeks usually don't conduct business without socializing. "Must you leave so quickly?" I asked. "Come in, drink some coffee," I urged. "I have work," she declined, and her forlorn figure dragged hastily away.

That year the demands of my house restoration prevented me from working onions for anyone. But a few seasons later I had more time, and I wanted to participate in the harvest. I knew that a broken ankle had incapacitated Lambi Houlis' wife Voula and that a labor shortage was drawing several gypsy families to Elika. I offered to work for Lambi in exchange for cement, and he agreed.

At noon the next day, I went by foot to Lambi's onion

field on the Marathia road—I had photographed the shepherd Theodhoris hand-shearing sheep in the morning. I anticipated finding Lambi and his workers leisurely eating home-cooked food from Tupperware containers in the shade of an olive tree. But when I arrived, Lambi and Rinoula—there were just the two of them—drove the chartreuse Nissan back to Lambi's house for dinner, and they took me with them. I had already eaten an egg, tomatoes, homemade bread, and his own cheese with Theodhoris, but to avoid a fuss, I ate again—in the confines of Voula's kitchen.

Within an hour we were back in the field, and I joined the onion pulling. Lambi had irrigated at dawn, and the moist soft earth yielded readily when I yanked the onions by their tube-like leaves. The local bird population compensated for Rinoula's and my quiescence.

A few mornings later the chartreuse Nissan appeared at my rental at eight, and Lambi again drove me to his onion field. When we arrived, the rollers of the leaf-cutter were already turning, and two women from Ay Mammas—a girl and her mother—were heaping onions into empty red, orange, and blue plastic crates and carrying them to the tractor-powered machine. Little Soula's father, Lambi, and Rinoula's husband, Nikos, arrived about the time we did. Little Soula's father took over the job of carrying to the machine the crates we women had filled. Nikos stood on a platform and dumped the onions into the receiving box. Lambi, our boss, stood at the back of the machine and controlled the flap that directed the flow of leafless red onions into pink net bags. At one point I yelled to Lambi, "How goes it, Boss?" He shouted back, "*Tak, tak, tak*—hurried work."

We finished by noon. The smell of diesel exhaust had

nauseated me slightly, and the engine drowned out any natural sound. But the mechanical cutter—one of several in Elika—had saved hours of labor. I wondered what explained the worker shortage.

The next day, a Saturday, Lambi and his son Dhimitris picked me up at noon. Lambi was fuming—his wife's injury and the worker shortage were prolonging his harvest and, before he finished getting his crop out of the ground, the price of onions had fallen from sixty drachmas a kilo to an appalling thirty drachmas.

Lambi's spirits improved once we set to work pulling onions again, but my mood deteriorated. Wind and the blazing afternoon sun had hard-baked the earth. Working on my knees, I routed the onions from the abrasive clay with my fingers, and when the bulbs were too deeply embedded to grasp, I freed them with well-aimed chops with a *skalistiri*—a miniature hoe. Hostile weeds scattered through parts of this field pricked my bare fingertips mercilessly. In spite of the juicy sweet oranges Lambi had picked for our refreshment, onion pulling had lost its romantic appeal.

I ended the workday stiff as the wooden handle of my *skalistiri* and thirsty as the parched earth. Lambi and I washed the dirt off our stained hands with the last of the water in his Styrofoam-insulated jug. We collected our *skalistiria*, I picked up the cellophane cookie wrappers Lambi had dropped on the ground, and we walked to the roadside. There we caught a ride to Elika in the back of someone's red pickup. Dhimitris, who was teaching elementary school in Neapolis during the week, had dropped us at the onion field before driving the chartreuse Nissan on to the nearby town of Sikea for an afternoon on the soccer field.

much work, nothing else

"Come," Ksanthi called when she saw me walking down the street the morning after I had cut onions for Lambi. She was climbing into a tractor wagon that would take her and several other hands to the driver's onion fields. Her message sounded more like a greeting than an invitation, so I answered, "Good day." "You tired yourself yesterday," she reported. "Yes, I cut onions for Lambi," I said. "I know," she smiled. "I sat all winter; my body was not accustomed to the work," I explained. "I picked olives all winter; I've been cutting onions for twenty days now," she replied. "I have not sat at all, and my body has not stopped aching."

After a pause, Ksanthi turned to the other women in the trailer and clapped her hands together as she announced, "She and I are the same age." "Which is more beautiful?" someone bantered. "We both are," I volunteered. "Did you hear?" Ksanthi laughed. "She said, 'We both are!' But she looks like a girl, and we get old," she demurred.

Ksanthi's observation reminded me of a comment she had made a few years earlier when I had stopped by her *baka-*

liko one evening during the onion harvest. "How is it going?" I asked. "Much work, nothing else," she moaned. I understood. In 1983 during interviews I conducted with the help of an Athenian woman off season during off-peak hours in her *bakaliko*, Ksanthi had told me about life in the onion fields.

Ksanthi plants two *stremmata*—two thousand square meters—of land her mother gave her. She harvests about seven tons of onions, which, in 1983, brought approximately seventy thousand drachmas. When she subtracts the costs of a tractor she hires to plow, irrigation water, fertilizer, and herbicide, her earnings amount to nothing. "Oil brings a steady income, but the onions, no," she explained.

I asked Ksanthi why she continues to plant onions when her profit is meager and unpredictable. "We don't like to stay at home; we women prefer to be in the fields." She added that because their *cafenio* and *bakaliko* do so little business in the winter when everyone works in the fields all day, the stores do not bring in enough money. Her husband is from Athina and does not know agricultural work, so he keeps the two stores during the day and Ksanthi works her own and other fields in a labor exchange system called the *apalaitika*. She also works for day wages in and around Elika.

"What should I do?" Ksanthi asked. "It pleases me; I like it. When I go to the fields, I make more money than if we both stayed in the shops. The people here in Elika have learned to shop at the *bakaliko* in the morning from seven until eight o'clock before we leave for the fields and in the evening after five when we return from the fields.

"I close the *bakaliko* at nine o'clock in the evening, and I go to the house and work. I clean, I wash clothes, and I cook. I cook the evening meal and for the next day so my husband will have something to eat. I don't have free time, not even on Sunday. This life we speak of, we don't have all year—only during the olive and the onion seasons. If we had the same amount of work all year, we wouldn't be able to endure. It's very tiring work."

The fact is, Ksanthi does have almost the same amount of work year round. Besides summer gardening and the winter olive harvest, onions require a sixteen-month-long round of toil. Seeds are sown in March. In August, miniature onions called *kokaria* are harvested. These are dried and stored until December or January when they are planted. Smaller *kokaria* yield onions that are pulled, cut, bagged, and marketed in July. Larger *kokaria* produce seed that is collected about the same time. Because of the unusually long growing cycle, a second generation of onions must be planted before the previous generation has produced seed!

Ksanthi plants, weeds, pulls, and cuts onions. "Planting *kokaria* is the most exhausting work," she told me. In the morning about ten women gather, depending on the size of the field. When they arrive, the one whose field they will work customarily treats the others to a sweet she has made. Ksanthi usually bakes a cake or *kourambiedhes,* and she takes along candies and gum from her *bakaliko.*

After the treat, the women get to work. When they plant *kokaria,* they work side by side, one woman about a meter away from the next. "Planting *kokaria* is exhausting because all day we are kneeling. Our backs ache, and our knees. Only at midday we all sit and eat. Each one has her food, and one tastes the food of the others. In the old days, the boss had the food and fed everyone. More recently, each one brings her own.

"One-half hour for food and afterwards, again work. When we work, we talk simultaneously. If someone knows village news, she tells the others. We gossip, we make puns, we tell jokes, we sing. We pass the time beautifully."

Ksanthi enjoys the company of the other women when she plants *kokaria,* and she tolerates the work. "We live from this; whether we like it or not, we go. We know however that planting the *kokaria,* we will make money later. If we sit at home—nothing. We won't have money."

About a month after they plant *kokaria,* the women gather again to weed. During the first weeding—kneeling again—they chop with a *ksistri,* a tool like the *skalistiri* but smaller. Ten to fifteen days later if weeds reappear, the women re-assemble and pull them out by hand. "When we see a lot of weeds, anguish takes hold of us," Ksanthi told me, "because weeding is tiring work. It is less tiring when they spray with herbicides. Everyone sprays now because if we didn't, many weeds would come up, and we would have to busy ourselves for fifty days to remove the weeds.

"The spray is very good. In the past, everyone struggled much more. But if you are not careful and you use too high a concentration, the onions will dry and you will not be able to sell them. Otherwise, the chemicals don't harm the onions because after we spray, they stay in the earth for three months. The chemicals have left the onions when we pull them.

"The chemical box has a skull. If by chance someone drinks a little of the chemical, it will poison him. People have committed suicide in many places from agricultural chemicals. But what can we do? All garden foods—beans, tomatoes—they spray them all, and everyone eats them. The point is, without herbicides we have to remove the weeds by hand.

And if you don't spray, the produce has worms."

The villagers tolerated blighted produce when they only grew for home consumption, but produce grown for sale has to meet market standards. "In the old days," Ksanthi explained, "they had only oil—olives. Now, recently, we have onions, too. Life demands it. We want to live well here in the village. We want our washing machines, our refrigerators. As they live in the capital, the people want to live here."

After the women plant and weed the onions, each farmer casts ammonium fertilizer, and then in March irrigation begins. Ksanthi's onion field does not have water so, like many other farmers, she purchases it. She pays by the hour for water piped to her field. "The water does not go by itself; you have to open an earth dam for the water to enter a little plot. After it fills, you have to close that dam and open another one so the water can enter the next plot. The water runs fast, and continuously one must cut dams. For my onions, I need five hours to irrigate, and I irrigate every five to six days. It is extremely wearisome."

After Ksanthi has irrigated eight times, her onions are ready to harvest. Up until the time I interviewed Ksanthi, onions were cut exclusively by hand. The women gathered again. They pulled the onions from the ground and laid them in rows with the leaves running parallel to the row. About ten days later when the leaves had dried, the women began to cut. The worker sat on the ground, her legs straddling the end of a pile. She planted a sickle handle in the ground between her knees; the cutting edge of the blade faced away from her. Reaching, she grabbed several onions from the pile, drew the leaves across the blade at the base, left the leaves in heaps for goat fodder, and sacked the onions. The men combined half-full bags, tied them, and loaded them in trucks for market.

"There is no pleasure when we cut onions; it does not exist," Ksanthi insisted. "It is excessively hot in May and June. In the winter when we plant *kokaria* it is very cold; either it rains, or it is cold. In the summer, we wear hats; we take cold water with us, or refrigerated orange juice.

"Cutting onions is tiring, and it is dangerous. When the onions are drying, scorpions gather. Because of this, we must cut cautiously so they won't bite us—the bite hurts very much." To protect themselves from the scorpions, the women tucked long trousers into their socks, in spite of the heat, and they wore gloves so the scorpions could not bite and so their hands would not reek of onions. Some women refused to wear gloves, and even with extreme vigilance, someone always got bitten. Even with the antidotes the women carry to the field, the bites are intensely painful for hours.

More rarely, someone is bitten by a deadly poisonous adder nesting in the dry leaves. "If you pull the onions and cut them quickly, the scorpions and snakes don't have time to gather," Ksanthi observed. Because the mechanical onion cutter cuts the leaves while they are still green, it reduces the risk of scorpion and adder bites. The first machine came to Elika from Thiva in 1983, the year I interviewed Ksanthi. "It is a great convenience. We throw the onions with the leaves on the machine, and it cuts the leaves off. The machine is a good solution because many times you don't find hands. People don't want to work any longer because agricultural work is tiring. Many times husbands don't want their wives to go to the onion fields. And the men are not able to sit on the ground all day, they say to vindicate themselves."

The youth disdain agricultural work, too. "The youth prefer especially to be workers in a factory in Athina rather than to stay in the village. My own children don't even want to stay at the stores we have. Very few youth stay in the village; they all leave. They only like the summer here to swim in the sea, to enjoy themselves. They don't want to winter here.

"When they finish elementary school, they leave. They go to Neapolis where there is a junior and a senior high school, and they stay there three to six years. My younger son wanted to go to technical school, but a technical school doesn't exist in Neapolis or in Sparti. And my older son wanted to go to the university. For this reason, they were compelled to go to Athina.

"I want my sons to study in Athina because I don't want them to have my life. Work in the fields is tiring; I want them to live better. But there are many expenses, so I struggle for my children and endeavor.

"Life here is very hard—the fields, the olives. We make produce, and we are unable to sell it at a good price. We fatigue ourselves without reward. In the village, life is beautiful in the summer. The winter is a tragedy; I don't like it at all."

tasty bread

One evening I went to Lambi Houlis' house to translate a letter his wife Voula had written to an English-speaking relative in America. Before Voula gave me the letter she insisted on serving me dinner, which included a slice of her own delicious oven-baked bread. I ate, and I translated the letter, and I was sitting by the fire when Rinoula's husband Nikos stopped by. Motivated by a rainbow that had bridged two rainstorms that day, I asked Nikos whether he customarily acknowledges the beauty around him or whether he has eyes only for work. "The second," he answered. "Like today, we worked all day; we didn't have time to see anything."

After Nikos left, I turned to Voula's neighbor Andriana, who was sitting with us. "Is it the same for you, or are you romantic?" I asked. She looked up from her crocheting. Stars glittered in midnight eyes. "Every day I look, and every day I see," she smiled. "It has been that way all my life."

Mihail's late brother-in-law Yiorgos Maravelias and my friend Vasiliki share Andriana's romantic spirit. Yiorgos was a career army officer who lived in Athina. When he retired, he spent long periods of time in his native Elika. He picked olives every season for the simple pleasure of it. And, like the farmer who used to make everything by hand, he built tables from circular slate slabs mounted on tripod limbs he cut from trees, and he made lamp shades from gourds.

Vasiliki writes poetry. Her passion for Beethoven and fine porcelain is no stronger than her urge to spend magical hours alone in an isolated mountain *kalivi*. Like Yiorgos, she flourishes during the olive harvest. And like him, she recalls the pleasures of the annual wheat harvest in the old days. "I want to tell you," Vasiliki stated, "that money does not always bring happiness."

■

Each winter before Vasiliki's father began to sow his fields in wheat, he broke a large pomegranate beside his seed supply. "It was the custom in the old days," Vasiliki told me, "to bring luck with the sowing."

God willing, in June, Vasiliki's family reaped many bundles of wheat and built a tall haystack beside the threshing floor adjacent to my house in Maravelianika. Since the first mechanical thresher arrived in Elika in 1956, most of the threshing floors have one by one been dismantled, but there used to be many of these floors scattered around Elika. Yiorgos recalled two in Maravelianika, four in Kokkinitsa, five or six in Kousoulianika, and others on the outskirts of the village.

The threshing floor is a circular expanse twelve meters in diameter paved in slate and delineated by a ring of standing slates. When the time came for a farmer to thresh, he threw all the bundles from his haystack across the threshing floor. Then eight to ten farmers led their plow animals onto the floor. They hitched the animals together side by side and harnessed the row to the center post. For one or two days, depending on the amount of wheat and its brittleness, the animals revolved around the post. The farmers who prodded the animals from behind outsang the birds. "The threshing was very beautiful," Vasiliki remembers.

When the hooves had cut up the wheat, the farmers heaped it into a pile to one side of the threshing floor. Before they began winnowing, they staked their handmade wooden pitchforks and shovels at the summit of the wheat pile. Vasiliki can still picture her father opening the bottle of oil her mother brought to the threshing circle and spilling the oil at the base of the pile in the form of a large cross. "It was symbolic for the people to nourish themselves with pleasure," Vasiliki explained.

After consecrating the wheat, the farmers sometimes waited five or ten days for the wind that would separate the chaff from the grain—not a north wind, but a strong sea breeze. While they waited for this sea breeze, the farmers asked for fair weather. "Many times it did rain when the wheat was on the threshing circle—anguish. Anguish because we relied on this wheat to pass the entire year."

When the strong sea breeze did come, Vasiliki's father and mother and uncles and aunts and cousins threw the wheat into the air with the shovels and pitchforks. "It was lovely. Quickly, quickly everyone threw. The chaff formed an enormous pile downwind, and the grain fell in place. If the wind blew steadily, they finished quickly because there were so many hands."

Once the wheat had been winnowed, the farmer was obligated to distribute shares before he took the remainder
home. He gave the priest a share because he had no crop of
his own. The haystack warden—who guarded twenty-four
hours a day against fire and theft—took his share. And the
blacksmith took a percent because all year he had repaired
and sharpened the farmer's plow.

When the distribution was complete, Vasiliki's father
shoveled his grain into sacks her grandmother had woven
from linen she cultivated, and he carried it home on his
packsaddle. He stored the grain in a large wooden chest that
sat in the kitchen.

"The chaff," Yiorgos told me, "they transported to the
hayloft in a beautiful way—and romantic." All the neighborhood girls and boys gathered together at the threshing
floor in the evening. They spread out large handwoven
sheets. Using pitchforks, the boys filled them with chaff.
Then they helped the girls take them on their backs to the
farmer's hayloft. "In this way contact between the girls and
the young men happened. They met and they spoke, and it
was a pleasurable evening for everyone because at the end
when they transported the chaff, they ate together at the
farmer's house, and afterwards they danced and sang and
played games. In that way they passed the evening very en-
joyably. All this did not happen one time, but every time a
farmer threshed wheat at the threshing floor."

The chaff did more than feed the animals in winter. "In
those days luxurious mattresses such as we buy today did
not exist," Vasiliki reminisced. "My mother had handwoven
fabric which she sewed herself and filled with clean chaff,
and we used this for a mattress. We put it on top of the chest

where we had our wheat. On top of the mattress we put a clean rag rug, and over that a clean hand-loomed sheet and a pillow which was also stuffed with chaff. There we slept. Every year we threw out the old chaff and replaced it with new so the mattress would be fresh. Practically speaking, it was very clean and very warm in the winter. You slept very softly.

"And there weren't bakeries like today that have everything. You had to have your own wheat in order to eat. With the first flour my father brought from the mill, my mother made *kourambiedhes* or *melomakarouna* (honey macaroons) to sweeten us, and afterwards she baked bread. All the houses had ovens; a house without an oven didn't exist then because every housekeeper baked."

Vasiliki's mother baked eight loaves of bread every Saturday. She rose before dawn and kneaded her dough on a *sofra* (a low round wooden table). When she had worked the dough well with her hands, she divided it and set it in the eight compartments of her rising box, which she had lined with a long narrow handwoven cloth. She covered the rising box with another clean ironed cloth and then other covers to protect the loaves while they rose. When the loaves were swollen with gas, she poked a hole in each one and ignited the branches in her oven. When the oven heated, she baked.

"Making bread required much toil," Vasiliki concedes, "but it was very tasty."

here and there

"In the old days," Fofoula told me, "people went to America very freely; they only had to have their tickets. They left Greece continuously because there existed great poverty; people didn't even have bread to eat. In America, my father became acquainted with my mother, they married, and my two older brothers were born in America—in New Jersey.

"My parents returned to Elika in 1918; my brothers then were eight and six years old. My grandfather was a priest and had land in the village. All his children were in America, and they agreed that someone had to return to keep the estate. My father preferred to go. He bought the tickets secretly, and when he told my mother, she said, 'I will work to repay you for the tickets, and we will stay in America.' She liked America very much and always had in mind returning. She died with this yearning.

"Four years after my parents returned to Elika, I was born, and then three other children. My two older brothers cried every day to return to America, but my father did not want to go. When my older brother turned eighteen he left for America, and later my other brother went.

"After my brothers left I was the oldest at home, and I looked after my three siblings. My parents preferred to leave me at the house because if they took me to the fields, I didn't work. I was lazy. I didn't like the fields. I didn't like the sun. I didn't like the cold. I was only able to pick olives a little. Many times when my parents took me with them I said my tooth ached, my stomach, my head. And they said, 'Leave, go to the house to sleep.'

"I left, I found my girlfriends, we made coffee, snacks, Turkish delight. At the time when I knew my parents would return I went to the house, and when they asked me how I was, I told them, 'I'm better; my stomachache has gone now.'

"I was fifteen, seventeen years old then. Afterwards my mind became more serious. When my parents returned they found food ready. I washed. I baked. I went three times a day for water—I liked to go for water because I met my girlfriends. If we were late, our parents came and hit us with a staff. I wove. I embroidered. When I was eighteen, I learned to sew in Neapolis—a sister of my father took me into her house, and another woman taught me to sew on a foot-pedal machine. I paid for my lessons with oil. I had gone to elementary school for six years, but they didn't send girls to high school—they sent the boys in my day."

In 1949 when Fofoula was twenty-seven, she married Petros. "I married late because there was war, and they didn't have weddings then. My father chose my husband; he received a proposal, and then my father asked me. The whole village said Petros was the most handsome young man. He was tall; he had a handsome face; he was strong, quiet. He was young—eight years older than me. But I told my father I would answer him in a month. My father said to me, 'If you want, all right. If you don't, it doesn't matter to me.' I observed Petros at the church, at festivals. I said afterwards that he was good, and the village said, 'Congratulations! You took a good young man.'

"I told my husband I didn't like field work, and he said, 'It doesn't matter; I don't want to take you to the fields. I want you to be at the house so you won't tire much and so I find everything ready when I return in the evening.'" So Fofoula stayed at home and raised two daughters and a son, and with the income from the land he received as dowry, Petros was able to hire workers to help him. Even so, manual labor tired Petros, and he asked his brothers-in-law to invite him and Fofoula to America. "I had a good image of America," Fofoula told me. "When my brothers visited us from America, I saw that they were very different from us. We were more tired. It appeared that they lived better. We liked their clothes; we weren't able to have so many clothes. They brought us summer and winter clothes. They brought us a few sheets. Everything was beautiful, and they told us that these things were not expensive in America."

In 1966, Fofoula and Petros left their children with their grandmother in Elika and went to America with the intention that, if they liked it, they would stay. They worked in a factory that made men's clothing, but were paid little. Fofoula found the work boring and tiring because she was standing for hours and she didn't know the language. "The third day after the factory hired me, I made a serious mistake. The foreman told me to cut a thread from the buttons that the machine had sewn. I didn't understand, and I thought he told me they had sewn the buttons by mistake. The buttons were on jackets for Vietnam soldiers, and a truck had arrived to transport them. I had cut the buttons off twenty jackets, and while they loaded them, they saw those that were missing the buttons. They asked the boss why they didn't have them. I saw the foreman carrying the jackets toward me, and he threw them on my table. The foreman slapped my head with his hand and said to me, 'Stupid! I told you what to do, and you did something else.' I was frightened. It hurt me, and I cried. He told me to leave, but another Greek woman who had worked there for years told him, 'She won't do it again. Tell me the instructions, and I will tell her.' And in that way, I didn't make another mistake.

"One day when I went to the factory, I slipped on the snow, fell on my back, and hit my hand. I cursed Columbus who discovered America. I said, 'Cuckold Columbus, who arrived with ragged underpants in America and took the people by the neck!' They heard me and wrote what I said to Elika. The winter was bad, but I liked everything else in America. I am still nostalgic, and I will go again to America to visit."

Fofoula liked the conveniences in America—the houses, the shops, the streets. But she was sad to be away from her children because they were young. Her older daughter was fourteen, her second daughter was eleven, and her son Lambi was another three years younger. The children asked her to come back, so after one year Fofoula returned from America to serve them.

Petros had to stay in America because he had rented their land in Elika and had sold their animals. But he liked life in America better than Fofoula did; work in a textile factory tired him less than farm work in Greece. "My husband said,

'There isn't another country like America.' On Sundays, he washed dishes; he worked every day of the week. He worked hard for twelve years because it paid and because we wanted to change our children's lives for the better. It was a very hard life in the village."

Within two years after Fofoula's return to Elika in 1967, water and electricity became available locally. Fofoula equipped their house immediately with water taps, lights, an iron, an oven, a refrigerator. "I knew about electricity because I had gone to America, but many old people who had not seen electricity crossed themselves and said, 'How beautiful these times are! We lived in darkness, in pitch.' Many women went outside and called, 'I bought a refrigerator! Come see how beautiful it is!' Another said she bought an iron, and it irons beautifully. Everyone was happy because they had not seen these things. My mother-in-law was an old woman, and she lived in our house. She said, 'How do you heat your iron, Daughter-in-Law?' I said, 'I plug it in, and it heats.' She couldn't understand. The old ones who saw gave their blessings to the inventor. Many thought electricity was a miracle."

In 1970 after her older daughter finished high school, Fofoula took Eleni to Athina to take examinations for teaching. They lived in the house Fofoula and Petros had built there. "We bought the lot in 1964, and we finished building in 1967. We built the house in Athina because we had a little money; we had to invest securely for our children. We didn't want to buy more fields because we had fields in Elika. Anyone who had money then bought in Athina because Athina had everything it has today—electric light, water. You could have central heating in your house. Athina had high schools and technical schools."

Shortly after they moved to Athina, Eleni met her husband at a relative's house. She married him in 1971, and the house in Athina became part of her dowry. That same year, Fofoula and Petros bought the adjoining lot and eventually built a second house for their other daughter Miroula's dowry. When Fofoula returned to Greece in 1967, she intended to stay. But Miroula did not want to attend high school, and she told her mother she wanted to go to America to be with her father. "If I like it," Miroula said, "I will stay." So in 1971 Fofoula left her son with Eleni in Athina, and she took her seventeen-year-old Miroula to America.

Fofoula worked in a factory that made scissors, pliers, and hammers. "It was very noisy from all the machinery. It was unhealthy work because we breathed the dust from the machines, and when we spit, we spit soot. But I wasn't able to find other work, and I liked to help the family."

Fofoula worked in the factory for four years. She liked America better the second time because she had time to adapt. She learned enough English to be able to shop by herself for whatever she wanted, and she got to know more Greek women with whom she kept company on the weekends. Her work was unpleasant, but she made more money.

Miroula also worked in a factory. She earned a good wage, but she didn't like it. She wanted to return to Greece to marry because she admired her sister's life in Athina; Eleni didn't work outside the house. Too, Miroula didn't know any young men in America, but she had many suitors in Greece. Eleni urged Miroula to return to Greece so they could be together, and Fofoula brought her back in 1975.

After Fofoula returned to Greece the second time, Miroula married in Athina. Fofoula could have stayed with her daughters in the capital, but she liked the village better. "I go very often to my daughters' homes in Athina and I am pleased, but I can stay only twenty, twenty-five days. The crowds in Athina tire me, and the traffic. And I have to go up on the roof to see the stars in the sky, to breathe. I rest better at my house in the village. I like the sea, the air, the peaceful life. I live with nature. I like it. I would like to live the rest of my life here in the village.

"And if you ask my daughters, they will tell you that it is a better life in the village. They come to Elika three times a year: Christmas, Easter, and the summer. But their husbands are unable to leave their work. One son-in-law works in an O.T.E. office [telephone office], and the other is a merchant. They have their salaries, and they don't know farm work—they have studied. My daughters miss their village, and they think that when their children are provided for, they will return to live like me in Elika. But my daughters say they don't want to turn back."

do you remember the horse?

"Do you remember the horse?" Nikos asked. Wanting to wash away a noon-hour thirst on the last day of May 1988, I walked over to my favorite Marathia *taverna*, the seaside *taverna*, to order a cool drink. I saw Kostas, who frequently invited me to join him for coffee, and sat down at his table.

Kostas was sitting with a companion. I did not recognize Nikos at first, partly because his razzle-dazzle American ice cream upstaged him, and partly because it had been a year since I had last seen him, and his appearance had changed abruptly during that time—he had grown into manhood.

Kostas and I chatted off and on while people on the move came and went. When Nikos interjected his question about the horse, I turned to Kostas and asked, "Do *you* know the horse?" He nodded yes. Then I looked back at Nikos and replied "Yes, I remember the horse." That was the extent of Nikos' and my conversation. The horse he referred to was his father's horse, a glistening dark Trojan that had been treated well in appreciation for its service. But I interpreted Nikos to mean, "Do you remember the *story* about the horse?"

On the eighth of November, the day after the 1982 olive season began, I set out early to photograph the morning exodus to the olive groves. Shortly after I stationed myself at the top of an agricultural road leading out of Elika, Nikos' father Panayotis came by. I assumed that he and his wife, who accompanied him on another horse, were going to their olive trees to pick, and I asked to accompany them. It had not occurred to me that I would gather olives for the first time in my life that day—I had dreamed of participating in the harvest ever since my first visit to Elika in 1974. But I thought I might observe the process.

Panayotis was glad for me to join up, but he knew that his trees were some distance away, and my reputation as an inveterate walker had not yet spread, so he wouldn't have me on foot—he insisted I ride with him. Without anticipating the consequences, I climbed onto the packsaddle. Mind you, we shared a seat designed for one. I was seated dangerously close behind him with my arms boldly wrapped around his waist. All this in full view of his wife who mutely plodded along behind. When I saw Zoe later that day, she had already heard via the grapevine about my shameless intimacy with Panayotis. The story had sent a wave of giggles through the village.

But Nikos' question had more to do with his memories of Panayotis than this story about Panayotis' horse and me. What he really was asking me was, "Do you remember my *father?*" By a traditional ceremony at the graveyard chapel in only a few days—June the third—villagers would commemorate the first anniversary of Panayotis' tragic death, the memory of which still pierced Nikos' heart and predominated his silence. He had witnessed his father's death. He watched helplessly as Panayotis' tractor—not yet a week old—overturned on a slope, rolled over Panayotis, and crushed him to death. Ironic that a labor-saving machine brought a premature end to his work life—he was not fifty years old. Ironic that the horseman died, not the soon-to-be obsolete horse. The horse was sure-footed. Panayotis trusted his tractor too much.

Yes, I remember Panayotis. I even remember the rough-grained leather patches sewn onto his work boots—something I noticed the time we rode together. But most indelibly I remember seeing him—teamed with his horse—running his plow at sunset, and later, on that same horse, clipping homeward. Yes, I remember Panayotis. Yes, I remember the horse. Panayotis and the horse were one.

orphans

Mihalis Grigorios Tsigounis seemed agitated. He smoked incessantly and paced the veranda. But when his wife Eleni asked, "Mihalis, why do you worry so much?" he would not answer. She sensed what the problem was, but did not let on. Instead, she repeated her question. At last he told her, "I have a great worry. The largest estate in the area is for sale, and because I've lent out so much of my cash, I don't have enough to make the purchase." The few-hundred-acre estate had water and numerous olive trees. It belonged to the Nikolaos Ritsos family, a wealthy family in Monemvasia who, along with the Capichinis, had acquired all the richest land in Lakonia from the Turks after liberation. Lust for gambling, women, and luxury had drawn the family to Athina. It lost control of the estate and gradually sold it off. Ritsos wanted the equivalent of one hundred eighty thousand kilos of oil for the tract Tsigounis wanted to buy—one hundred forty-five thousand drachmas, an unthinkable sum at the time.

Three other men had joined forces and vied for the estate. Although one of them apparently had minimal resources, the second could almost meet the purchase price. The third man was a distant relative of Mihalis Grigorios Tsigounis, and he intended to borrow the difference from him. He boasted at the *taverna*, "My cousin Mihalis will cast his gold into a plow to turn the earth, and I will have the land." Tsigounis caught wind of the boast, and when the man arrived to take the loan, he turned him away.

This did nothing to alter Tsigounis' own shortage of cash. When his wife asked how much money he required, he refused to speak. Finally, when she insisted, Tsigounis revealed the amount. He needed seventy thousand drachmas. "Wait a minute," Eleni said. She disappeared into the cellar and returned with seventy thousand drachmas—money she had accumulated from the sale of almonds, oranges, and cheese, as well as unspent household money. She gave him the drachmas, Tsigounis purchased the land, and both husband and wife were happy. That was in 1917. Mihalis Grigorios Tsigounis was Mihail's grandfather.

Mihail never knew his grandfather because he died in 1928, a year before Mihail's birth. But Mihail heard stories about him all his life. In 1954 when he started running the family olive oil factory, Mihail installed a more efficient oil separator. Afterwards, he traveled to neighboring villages to encourage them to modernize their factories. Even then, sons of men who had received long-term, low-interest real estate loans told Mihail stories about his grandfather. As long as they lived, these old men expressed gratitude—with gift baskets of walnuts, oranges, and almonds—to Mihail for his grandfather's goodheartedness.

Mihail's grandfather was ten years old and orphaned when his father's brother brought him to Elika from Kythira, an island twenty-five kilometers off the coast of Neapolis. Papa Nikolas, who was Elika's first priest, raised grandfather Tsigounis and educated him through the ninth grade—an exceptional education at the time. When he finished school, his uncle helped him buy land, and because grandfather Tsigounis worked intelligently and diligently, he accumulated money and bought more land. Eventually grandfather Tsigounis was in a position to take a wife from a wealthy family in Molaoi, the district capital. The marriage would have been arranged, as was the custom then, and the dowry of a girl from a family of means extended Tsigounis' estate.

The trees on Tsigounis' land eventually produced approximately forty thousand kilos of oil annually—a considerable volume at that time. In addition to marketing his oil Tsigounis marketed all the local wine, and his wife Eleni traded wool. By working hard and economizing, the couple raised eight children in a two-and-a-half-room house and kitchen, and they provided hospitality—bed and board—to the traders and officials traveling by foot or on horseback between Molaoi and Neapolis.

In due time, each of the four Tsigounis girls was married off with attractive sums of money and, in only one case, a piece of land. Of the four sons, two left the land. The second son married and lived in Athina where he traded olive oil and invested unwisely. The fourth son studied engineering and married in Germany, where he died prematurely. The other two sons remained by their father's side and worked the land in Elika. When Mihalis Grigorios Tsigounis died, he divided his estate among his three living sons.

Of the two sons who remained on the land, grandfather Tsigounis' first son, Theodhoros, worked longest and hardest.

He finished junior high school at age fifteen and tended his trees until six months before he died at age ninety-five. In the winter, he supervised sixty to seventy workers who collected the olives. (His wife Yioryia cooked midday meals for all of them.) In the spring, he shared his expertise with the ten to twenty workers who pruned with him. And twice annually, in the spring and in the fall, he hired fifteen teams of horses which, along with his own two teams, cultivated the olive groves.

In addition, Theodhoros improved his land by grafting olive trees. The olive, in wild form, is indigenous to the Peloponnese. It favors the mild Mediterranean winters. But the olives of a wild tree yield only a fraction of the oil produced by domesticated varieties. So Theodhoros imported domesticated shoots from Attica, where the olive was first cultivated, and he grafted them to wild root stocks, which he often transplanted to improve the distribution of trees on his land. The oldest trees he tended, with the help of workers, for nearly eighty years. All his trees he brought up like children.

Theodhoros Tsigounis and Yioryia raised four children, their son Mihail and three daughters. Two daughters married army officers who lived in Athina. The youngest married an oil merchant in Neapolis. Since none of their husbands lived and farmed in Elika, each daughter's dowry consisted of an apartment and the cash equivalent of land. When Theodhoros Tsigounis died in 1978, Mihail became the sole proprietor of his estate. Because neither of Mihail's two uncles produced heirs, he inherited their shares as well. Mihalis Grigorios Tsigounis' estate was reconsolidated in the hands of his grandson.

Mihail managed his land in keeping with the motto of his

time: less effort, more gain. In his father's day, workers most eager for profit went to the fields in the night; by hanging staffs, belts, scarves, or jackets in the branches, they claimed trees that stood on level ground and were heavy with fruit. Because they often had walked an hour or more to reach an olive grove, they frequently stayed, built fires, and talked or slept—sometimes in the rain—until morning. Workers who came later inevitably disputed the claims made by the early arrivers. Mihail stopped this system when, at eighteen, he began to supervise the land. Instead, the workers arrived with him at eight o'clock, and Mihail assigned trees equitably.

In his father's day, a worker picked olives by the handful and dropped them into a hand-loomed linen–and–goat hair *tagari* tied around the waist so that a stick could be set across the top to hold it open. Depending on the worker's appetite for profit, he collected up to twelve or fifteen kilos of olives in the sack before stopping to empty it. Mihail replaced this method with the comb-and-canvass system which had been developed elsewhere. Workers laid large ground cloths under a tree and used special plastic-toothed combs (like miniature garden rakes) to free the olives. The olives dropped onto the ground cloths, and when the entire tree had been picked, the fruit was sacked all at once.

The comb-and-canvass system, which is still used, spares the worker the weight of the waist sack, which was particularly uncomfortable to pregnant workers. (Some women used to pick olives when they were as much as seven or eight months pregnant.) Without the waist sack, all workers move more freely and safely in the branches and on the ladders. They collect more fruit more quickly—an economic benefit to them and to their employers. Also, the workers are less tired and quarrelsome. Until recently, their songs glided through the air all day long.

But for Mihail, managing a large estate became more and more burdensome in spite of the enviable lifestyle the income from his trees supported. Olive trees must be cultivated, pruned, fertilized, and, if possible, irrigated as well as harvested. This care requires vast amounts of energy and knowledge. Before World War II, manpower was available in Elika. Families usually raised seven, eight, or more children, yet they had not planted enough trees on their twenty to forty *stremmata* to support them. But they had time and extra hands to hire out, so labor was available to Tsigounis.

After the war, village populations began to decline all over Greece. Young men joined the merchant marine. Others went abroad, no longer to send dowry money home for their sisters, but to make their own fortunes. And increasing numbers of village youth moved to Athina. A scarcity of workers and the accompanying shortage of plow animals threatened the survival of large estates.

In response, Mihail bought a one-and-a-half-ton truck in 1956 and a thirty-five-horsepower Massey Ferguson tractor in 1958, and he promoted road building in the mountains. He transported workers, supplies, and the harvest in the vehicles. And he cultivated some land more efficiently with the tractor, although its glistening blades are insensitive to crucial shallow-growing olive roots. But many of Mihail's trees grow on terrain unsuitable for vehicles, so Mihail still needed a work force. As the labor shortage in Elika worsened, he hired people from neighboring villages. By the early 1960s, the shortage was so acute that Mihail recruited some thirty-five workers from villages as far away as Tripolis. He paid their bus fares and housed them locally. But after three years, an electricity plant in Tripolis preempted even these hands.

As a last resort, Mihail sold his inaccessible land and distributed his other land to village farmers on a long-term basis. They graze their stock and plant grains and vegetables freely. In the winter they take fifty percent of the olives they harvest.

The workers do not tend Mihail's trees with the skill that had become a Tsigounis tradition. And the inaccessible trees go untended and have grown wild. Mihail feels bereft. "The relationship between a man and a tree is very complex. When I go up to a tree to prune, I have the feeling of going to a beautiful woman. And when an olive tree is filled with fruit, it's a wonderful, wonderful picture. The individual form of the trunk; the shape of the branches bending under the weight of the fruit; the double color of the leaves, dark green on top and silver underneath; the color of the fruit, which starts as a soft green and turns pink and then perhaps purple as it ripens.

"The tree itself is beautiful, and it is beautiful because it gives a lot—the fruit for food, a delicacy. And wood for oven and hearth. And oil for cooking and healing. The ancients observed the miraculous effects of olive oil. For instance, Hippocrates stressed the use of olive oil combined with some herbs for wounds. And in modern times, I remember my grandmother making an ointment for burns from olive oil, beeswax, and herbs.

"And the olive branches, which provide shade for the tired workers at midday in the summer. In the same way, they used to lie down and talk in the shade of an olive tree in ancient Athina. Olive trees and maple trees grew in the *agora* where philosophers used to teach. When Socrates taught, he sat in the shade of a tree near the bank of the River Ilisos. And at the Academy of Plato was a famous olive tree that endured for more than twenty-three hundred years before a truck knocked it down. That was the Tree of Plato at Keramikos near Athina.

"And oil for ritual. Just like today, when the ancients entombed their dead, they anointed the bodies first and then consecrated the graves with oil. And they offered to their dead oil, wine, and kernels of wheat—the *spondhes*—exactly as we do today after twenty-five hundred years.

"Basically the tree is a kind of tradition. You know that your father, your grandfather, and perhaps your great-grandfather tended the tree, and that goes back a century or more. It reminds me of something I read—*To a God Unknown*. It was about a man who stayed on his father's land in spite of a drought. He stayed there because the tree personified the soul of his father. The tree talked to him like his father. I go sometimes to the olive grove, and that takes me back to my childhood when I followed my father to the orchard and he pruned or grafted. When I see the trees now, I think about my father. He had a straight character; he was very kind, very tender. He was thoughtful of people—not only people of Elika, but all people.

"When I was in close contact with them, I was in love with these trees, but not any more. Now I am just indifferent because there is nothing I can do for them."

■

Mihail's grandfather was a child without parents; he planted some trees. Mihail is a man without children; he orphaned an estate. To what extent were their lives governed by fate?

a real odyssey

The war between Greece and Italy that broke out in October 1940 found Mihail in Sparti, at the age of ten, attending junior high school. "I was living at our teacher's house, and because I was the only son in my family and I was spoiled by my mother and my three sisters, I was not satisfied there where I lived. I was anxious to leave. After a month of school, when the Italians assaulted our country, school closed up, so I had to leave and come home. The following year I went to junior high at Molaoi, but by then we already were slaves under the Germans and Italians. Can you imagine a little kid being faced with foreign soldiers after what he was taught about his history? It was a real trauma for a young patriot.

"However, I stayed in Molaoi for another two years. Then in the summer of 1943 the communist guerrillas came into this area, and we had to escape to save our necks. The communists were after my father because he refused to join them. He knew they were not patriots. They wanted him and everyone else who had influence on people. I forgot to say that in August 1941, a few months after the Italians came into

Lakonia, they took my father to prison for a year. They said he had given shelter to several British military and that he was hiding weapons. So they took him to prison in Yithion, originally, and then in Tripolis, and then in Patras—he was transferred from prison to prison. After a year he was pardoned because they didn't find any weapons, and they didn't catch my father directly giving aid or shelter to Allied soldiers or officers hiding in the area. He was released on Mussolini's daughter's birthday because the prisons were too full.

"My father came back home with feet swollen from the cold. He also had been beaten by the Italians. He was still recovering in bed when a communist leader tried to enlist him in their movement. My father knew better and said sharply, 'No, I've already given my share to the Resistance in prison. If I recuperate, I'll do whatever I have to do as a Greek and as a patriot but now, leave me alone.'

"From that moment, the decision had been made against my father; his sentence was death. A few months later the communists came to execute his sentence, but we were informed. Someone unknown to us at that time caught sight of a paper. He came directly by night and told my father and the others who were condemned to death by the communists to run, to hide someplace, to escape to Athina, anyplace to avoid execution.

"Immediately after that, I came home from a festival at a mountain chapel north of Neapolis. I was with a cousin of mine and Hariklia—the woman you rented your first house from—and her older brother who now lives in America. We reached the village around nine o'clock at night. I noticed that all the houses were closed. A very few people outside on the *agora* glanced at me in a suspicious way as I passed by on a donkey. I didn't know that they were communists, just that they were staring at me in a peculiar way.

"I reached my house. The door was locked; the window shutters were locked. All dark. The house looked mysterious to me. I knocked on the door two times. No answer. I knocked again. Suddenly my mother opened a window next to the door, waved her hand as if she was afraid of something, and asked who was knocking. 'It's me. Open up,' I said.

"Right away my mother opened the door, and then she closed it right away behind me. The house was half dark. Everything seemed spooky. I looked for my father. He didn't appear. I saw an old man, my father's cousin. He said my father was hiding. They told me the reason and said I had to go away immediately. I said, 'I'm hungry and tired. Give me something to eat and let me have a bed to sleep in for a while.' They said; 'No, you must leave immediately, unless you want to be caught and, along with your father, be put to death.'

"If the communists had caught me, they would have used me to find my father, and they would have killed us both. That is a fact. It is a sure thing that they would have done so, because that very same night they caught a sixteen-year-old boy, and they executed him. A year earlier, thinking that he was going to fight for his country, he had joined the communist guerrillas up in the mountains. When he realized that they were not going to fight for their country, he escaped and came down to the village again to try to tell people the truth. He was a brilliant boy with noble feelings—a patriot. But the local communists had condemned him to death, and at dawn on the sixteenth of August, 1943, that boy was executed outside my house.

"I had already left earlier that night. I left disguised in a woman's dress. My sisters and my cousin accompanied me out of the door and across the yard. I left the village, reached Marathia, and escaped by boat to Elafonisos, a small island offshore. I hid there for twenty days—the last five days sleeping in a cemetery where I waited for a boat to take me to my father.

"At last one night they came in a boat and took me to the cave near Neapolis where my father had been hiding. I met my father, whom I had suspected had been killed. You know how a young boy's mind would work—all those twenty days lying on the sand under a cedar tree near the water. I looked toward Elika because I imagined they would put the whole village to fire. Fortunately, they didn't. But I was imagining it.

"Anyway, they finally took me to my father. I hid there with him for two or three days, and then we were discovered. We were betrayed by a path carelessly made by the people who brought us food and water several times a day. A shepherd who crossed the path followed it to the cavern. Usually my father knew when somebody was coming because they whistled a signal from the distance. But that noon, no notice, no signal, and the bush to the cavern opened abruptly. Both my father and the intruder panicked. My father was expecting the guerrillas, who were in fact looking for us—forty of them were searching the area. And the intruder, a shepherd who was innocent of all that, found a pistol aimed at his face, poor man.

"After that, we had to leave the cave immediately for fear the people who brought us food—our relatives and friends— would be punished. In a quarter hour, we collected everything we had in four *tagaria*. We arranged everything to look as if no man had ever stayed there. And we ran to a thicket an hour away, where we hid. The next morning, very cautiously, my father went to notify his people, who meanwhile had discovered our disappearance and were worried.

"The following day, we met with Yiorgos Maravelias; he was a captain in the Greek army then, and later he married my sister. The three of us found a boat and rowed across the Lakonian Gulf to Skoutari, where my father's cousin Stavroula gave us hospitality before her son took us to Yithion. From there, about a month later, we made it to Athina. Our escape was a real odyssey!

"We stayed in Athina until independence, which came exactly a year later. We reached Athina in October 1943, and independence came in October 1944. When independence came, we learned about our mother. My father had been telling us that she stayed in the village to take care of the house and the land, and that the communists didn't touch her. In fact he knew that she had been taken up to the mountains.

"My father never believed that the communists would go so far as to put a hand on a woman, but they did, unfortunately. My sisters escaped to Athina and joined us, while my mother stayed back, alone. She was afraid of retaliation against her relatives if she left. She was caught and taken to the mountains for a year. She walked with the guerrillas from village to village and nursed them to save her life—a real hardship.

"When the country was liberated in 1944, she was released along with thousands of other hostages. After a few days, she came up to Athina and we all stayed there together. We didn't dare come back to Elika, regardless of independence. The communists were all over the country with weapons. We didn't want another adventure with them! So with thousands of other families from the provinces, we stayed in Athina. And that is one of the many reasons why people started liking the city and migrating there. The anonymity—they knew they would be faceless among the crowds in the city.

"Not long after independence—in a matter of two months—the December Coup broke out in Athina. It lasted forty-five days. There were fires, bombings of buildings, killings by thousands, especially in Athina. Churchill himself visited the capital on Christmas Day, 1944. The communists surrendered two weeks later when a Greek brigade, supported by some British regiments Churchill brought over, defeated them. Yiorgos Papandreou was reinstated as prime minister.

"But things did not stop there. Two years later, when I was sixteen years old, the second round of guerrilla warfare broke out, and we had the so-called Civil War against the communists, supported by the northern neighbors: the Yugoslavians, Albanians, Bulgarians, and of course the Russians behind them. After three and a half years, in the month of August 1949, the communists were again defeated. By that time I was nineteen years old.

"All those years, when a young fellow can enjoy life most because of his innocence and youth. All those years—what should have been the best years of my life—were spent with the eruption of machine guns, the crying of people, and seeing the dead."

the immortal homer

The colorfully striped rag rugs that carpet floors and uphol-
ster pickups throughout Greece chart the history of the
nation: the yellows, whites, and roses of peace, prosperity,
and knowledge; and the purples, browns, and grays of com-
bat, privation, and ignorance. The epic poetry of Homer
forms a warp that runs through every upheaval and resettle-
ment; it ties contemporary Hellenes to their ancestors. Even
during the black four-hundred-year-long Turkish Occupation, which ended in 1827, priests assembled youths in sub-
terranean church rooms with secret doorways and in caverns
with hidden entrances. There, along with Orthodoxy and
grammar, they taught the glories of Odysseus to inspire the
youth with hope for Greece's freedom.

Mihail is Elika's historian; he weaves references to Homer
into practically every discourse. One time Mihail told me the
story of a bandit who tried to rob his grandfather. This bandit
and reputed killer terrorized the northwestern Peloponnese
until the police killed his brother in a confrontation near Patras. The bandit, named Kostakos, jumped onto a ship and

migrated to America. There he lived the life of a gambler and gangster until the threat of the electric chair sent him back to Greece.

Kostakos had been advised that a large sum of cash lay hidden in a wooden closet in the home of Mihalis Grigorios Tsigounis in Elika, a small village in southern Lakonia. This Tsigounis was known for his profitable commercial transactions; Kostakos set his sights on Tsigounis' money.

For six months in 1911, Kostakos circled Elika in an effort to find access to Tsigounis' house. Tsigounis was informed of Kostakos' intent, but did nothing.

Then one day at noon, when Tsigounis was cultivating the orange grove next to his house with an ax, the bandit broke in. He and his two comrades who patrolled outside were armed to the teeth with pistols and daggers. Kostakos pinned Tsigounis' wife Eleni to the wall and threatened to kill her and her eight-year-old daughter if either one called for help. Then he set down his gun and began to force open the closet with a tool. Unintimidated, Eleni signaled her daughter to sneak out a narrow corridor and notify her father. Tsigounis kept no money in the closet, only papers. But because the bandit had invaded his family asylum to do harm, he took off his shoes and, with ax in hand, he tiptoed into the house, up the stairs, along the corridor, and into the room. Then he knocked Kostakos on the forehead with his ax before Kostakos had time to reach for his gun.

Tsigounis gave Kostakos a bed, and Eleni nursed and fed him for twenty days. Then when he was well enough to travel, his police guard escorted him to court. He was sentenced to fifteen years in prison.

When Kostakos was released, he returned to Elika and

asked Tsigounis to pardon him. Tsigounis did, and they shook hands and became friends. The following year, 1928, both men died.

Incidents like this were uncommon in those days, Mihail explained, and so reports of the attempted theft traveled not only throughout the county of Lakonia, but they reached Athina and even America. Thirty or forty years after the incident, a poet named Theodhoris from the village of Rihea passed through Elika and sang a ballad about Kostakos. He was blind like Homer, Mihail informed me, and his song echoed the rhythm of Homer's epic poetry.

Another time, I asked Mihail what kind of life it was for his mother and grandmother, both of whom provided beds and meals for those journeying to and through Elika. "Of course it was tiresome for a woman day after day, year after year for her whole life to work this way. Even if she could secure one or two girls to help her, she had to work herself in a cruel way.

"But you had to do it, because you couldn't leave people out in the rain or out in the night without food and shelter, and in those days Neapolis was a six-hour walk from here. Today people can afford to be indifferent—inhospitable—because there is always a hotel in the next town. But in those days, travelers had to stay overnight somewhere, and someone passing through stayed at our home practically every night. Usually they were government officials or merchants— in some cases even beggars. In most cases, these were good experiences. I remember one instance when my father provided hospitality, and two years later our lives were saved by the people he had given hospitality to.

"A woman, Stavroula, came on foot to our house from the

Mani on the other side of the gulf. It was the summer of 1941 before my father was captured by the Italians. I think she was a third cousin of my father. She was an old woman, and she came along with a young son of hers. She came for food. There was terrible famine in those days because of the war. People starved, especially in the cities and in the Mani because the land is so barren there. So the poor woman, not having food for her children, remembered my father who was a remote cousin, and she came asking for food. He gave her what she could carry on her shoulders because she didn't have an animal, and she had to walk for more than thirty hours to return to her village, Skoutari.

"Two years later, we left Elika because we knew the communists were after us. We crossed the gulf in a boat and landed near Skoutari around five o'clock in the afternoon. My father remembered this cousin Stavroula and walked inland to her village to bring water and to find transportation to Yithion—we had bedding, some food, and clothing. It was me, my father, and Yiorgos Maravelias. My father came back with water, and we bedded there on the rocky seashore.

"The following morning that woman's older son came down with a donkey, we loaded our things, and we started off. The walk to Yithion took four hours. On the road, we met six armed men who belonged to the local communist organization. The boy gave them an explanation, and we got through without harm. Later we heard that that young man was a communist, and those six men on the road were his friends. My father had told his cousin—the woman Stavroula—and her children of his peril. But regardless of the hatred and the passion of the communists, her son didn't give us up to his friends—perhaps under pressure from his mother, and also because of the tradition of hospitality, an ideal that goes back to Homer. I remember a passage from the *Odyssey* when the goddess Athina visited the house of Odysseus disguised as the merchant Mentes in order to advise Telemahos, the only son of Odysseus, to go to Nestor, King of Pylos and the oldest and wisest king participating in the Trojan War, and then to Menelaos, King of Sparti and husband of Helen of Troy, to ask about Odysseus' fate. 'Hail, Stranger! Here with us you shall be welcome, and when you have tasted food, you shall make known yourself.' All through the *Odyssey* and the *Iliad,* the same phenomenon is repeated. Whenever a stranger visited a household—king, god, or beggar—he was invited to the table to eat meat and bread and to drink wine. When his belly was full, his host would ask him to reveal his name and his destination. But imagine if that woman Stavroula never came to ask my father for food, and we went to the Mani to escape—we would easily have been killed!"

Yet another time I asked Mihail about water resources in Elika. He began by telling me about the mountain spring water that used to be collected in small reservoirs where his mother and sisters and other women and girls once filled their water jugs for drinking and cooking. Clothes were washed in rainwater collected in barrels at the houses in winter, he told me, but in the summer, women took the clothes to a stream to wash.

"I remember when I was a youth," he recollected, "my mother used to take me and my sisters on top of our horses and mules, which were loaded on the sides with baskets of clothing, sheets, and blankets. We went an hour away to a stream where we spent the whole day splashing around.

Meanwhile my mother and other women boiled water in big bronze pots and soaped and rinsed the clothes. Then they would lay all the clean clothes in the baskets, cover them with white linen, put branches of the myrtle bush on top, and pour hot water over them. What remains in my mind is the startling white of the linen and the aroma in the clothes. It was beautiful. And it is identical to the way Homer describes the young women washing clothes in the scene when Odysseus, who had been washed ashore, was awakened by the shouts of the girls playing at the stream where they washed their clothes."

Mihail referred so often to Homer that I asked him one time how Homeric tradition affects villagers who have not read the *Iliad* and the *Odyssey*. "Not everybody has read Homer," he concurred, "but practically everyone has something of Homer's wisdom. If you noticed the old woman last night when we dined at the *taverna* at Marathia—the old woman Irini. She started talking wisely in rhyme. And that is the case here. Many of the old people do that. This probably came down with tradition, and you hear unschooled people stating things that leave you astonished."

dancing girl

When I returned to Irini shortly after my arrival in Elika in the spring of 1990, her daughter Florentia accompanied me to her bedside. "You have company," she announced. "Company," Irini mimicked, eyes open but not seeing. I pulled a chair close to her bed, where she lay nestled as much like a child waiting to be born as an old woman hesitating to die. "It's Thordis," Florentia persisted. "Thordis," Irini groaned. In the adjacent room, her great-grandchildren romped in front of a blaring TV set. Irini's gnarled hand emerged from under the blankets and instinctively found mine. Her crooked fingers curled tentatively around mine and then withdrew. Irini's eyes closed, and in a little while I left her.

For the first time, Irini did not know me. But she was ninety-eight and had been preparing for her passage for years. When we first became friends, she was eighty-nine. Vividly I recall sitting around a table at Florentia's Marathia *taverna*—Irini, Florentia, Zoe and Mihail, and the priest Papa Nikolas and his two young sons. "I'm getting old," Irini quipped. "I will die soon." Then she turned a wizened face to the boys and said in a voice crackling with laughter, "When I die, I don't want mourners cloaked in black and peering like crows into my grave. They should wear red capes, make music, and dance."

■

I began herding sheep when I was nine, ten years old, and in the winter I wore a white woolen cape with a little hood. When I wore the cape and was in the midst of the sheep, I couldn't be distinguished from them. There among the sheep I danced. I sang. "Let my eyes see how my love is getting by. I hope he hasn't found another love and deserted me. *Opa!*"

When the weather became warm, we would take our flocks to our own fields on the slopes below the village. I would be alone then, and I'd dance by myself. I'd sing by myself. "I won't be going to Karava . . ." [Karava is a village on the island Kythira.] But all the flocks were together when we'd go to the mountains in the winter, and I had company. One time I was at Skopeles, and there was a shepherd at Heroma. I won't forget how this shepherd played his flute. I am an old woman—ninety years old—and still I remember; he played beautifully. I called him, "Come on, Smarty, if only I had your flute." He said to me, "Don't you like it?" And I told him, "I'm almost ready to dance. Do I like it!" I used to see him often. He sent his father to ask for me in marriage, but I didn't want a shepherd. I was seventeen, eighteen years old.

I liked the mountains because other children gathered with their animals and we herded together. We herded and we danced. One time we were at Skopeles; I had Areti with me. Areti grazed the sheep, and I was on top of the mountain. I had told her, "Areti, take the flock around." And she said, "Again I must herd the sheep?" She took them, and I climbed the mountain and viewed the sheep from up there. We had blackmailed Areti. One time from our hunger, we persuaded her to slaughter a lamb. "Kill the lamb. We won't tell your father." We convinced her, and she slaughtered it, and we cooked the liver. After that, we told her, "If you don't herd our sheep, we'll tell your father." We had good times.

I loved Areti; we were friends. Every morning we conferred: where shall we go today? And we came to an agreement so we could be together. Sometimes we quarreled; sometimes we danced. Then one took the flock; the other rested. We joined all the flocks—Areti's, Kaliopi's, and mine. We joined the three, and I was the king. Whatever I said, it happened. I said, "Now Kaliopi will herd the sheep. Now Areti will go . . ."

One time Areti climbed up an olive tree and wet on me. I was sleeping in the shade, and she climbed into the olive tree where I slept, and she pissed on me. I had told Areti, "I'm going to sleep, and you are going to take the flock." And she said, "My God, that you should sleep and have me herding the flock!" And I thought it was a bug and I kept wiping my face, and she started laughing from the tree above. No wonder I'm wrinkled now!

Every evening the other children returned to their houses in the village. They were *vikolounia* [literally, little ones who tended the oxen]. They had two or three oxen, a few goats or sheep, and donkeys. In the evening, they had to load wood on the donkeys. The *vikolounia* didn't have *kalivia*. But the shepherds stayed in *kalivia* in the mountains. I was a shepherd.

> I was a shepherd, an old shepherd,
> The mother of Ntaveli [a nineteenth century bandit].
> Shepherd, you shepherd, if I had your pants . . .

I stayed the whole winter in the mountains at Kourkoula. Now, there wasn't a *kalivi* at Kourkoula. My father made one. He put a pole in the center, and he wove reeds all around, and on top of them, mats. The mats came from the olive factory and had oil in them. The rain didn't pass through the mats. And all around the hut, my father dug a furrow so the water wouldn't go in when it rained. The hut had a little door; the rest was closed. We laid branches on the floor, and on top of them a rag rug, and I slept.

I'd go to the hut tired from herding the sheep, and damp. Those years, the winters were very cold and it rained. Many times I slept in damp clothes because I didn't have others to wear. I had my little rag dress, and over my dress, my white cape with a hood.

I stayed in the hut alone, and my brother came every evening—Angelis. My mother found Angelis; he was from another mother. When my ill-fated mother married my father, he had three children. Afterwards they had the four of us. I was born last, so there were years between Angelis and me.

When I was young, Angelis went to America. Later he returned and married. When he married he received ten sheep as dowry, and I herded them and made seventy. And Angelis brought food every evening. He brought greens, *pita*, beans.

Sometimes he brought *hilopita*—my mother made the pasta by hand. He brought me a little bread. He said, "Don't eat much bread tonight, Rinio. Eat your food so that in the morning you can take the bread with you."

Angelis brought me food, and then he left—he played cards in Ay Mammas. He played every night. The wolves howled, the foxes, and I trembled inside the hut. My brother returned at daybreak and told me, "Ill-fated One, don't tell our father that I go to Ay Mammas or I'll kill you." And I was afraid of him. My father thought Angelis stayed with me, but I was alone. So you see, in this way I passed the winter in a hut covered with mats, alone, at Kourkoula.

I didn't go home at all during the winter; I went every fifteen days. Angelis arrived and told me, "Mother said to come to the village and change." In the evening, I went. When I got home, my mother told me, "Again you brought your dress in rags, Rinio! Undress and sleep so I can patch it." If it was dirty she had to wash it, and in the morning I wore it again. I didn't have anything else to wear. I only had my hand-loomed dress and underclothes I knit from wool. When I grazed the sheep, I was knitting and spinning. My mother gave me puffs of wool to spin, and when I returned home, when I didn't have enough yarn on my distaff my mother spanked me.

I went home when the sun had set, and when I arrived, it was cold. My father said to me, "Come here, Rinio, and warm up." He loved me, woe be it. He took the *sofra* from the kitchen wall, and we sat on low stools by the fire and ate. My mother put beans or greens on a big plate, and she threw down mouthfuls of bread, my ill-fated mother, and all the children ate. How many were we? We were seven children. I was the youngest, and I admired the food, but I didn't get to it. My mother said to me, "You eat, too, Rinio. Woe be it, you remain without again."

In the morning when I took out the sheep, I had eaten my bread before the sun had risen—a piece of bread and two, three olives. I had nothing else, and all day I looked at the sun and said, "Sun, why don't you set?"

I herded the sheep, and I held my staff in my hand—my father made it. And when the sheep did damage, I hit them with the staff. I prodded them, and they left. But when they were hungry, they didn't stop for anything—they ran to find food. Like me when I saw in the distance a wild pear tree and I ran. And if the pears weren't ripe, I would throw stones at them because I was so hungry.

We used to eat wild pears and *koumara* [a small wild fruit]. We'd eat *koumara* when we were tending the flock, and then we'd cut twigs from the *koumara* and remove the leaves and pass the *koumara* on the twigs like *souvlakia*. We'd carry them to the village. My mother said to me, "Rinio, bring the children *koumara*."

In the spring when the sheep had milk, I chose the one that had the most milk, and I took a leaf from a fig tree and I milked into it. Then I dripped a little bit of fig milk from the leaf or from the fig before it ripened, and the milk curdled. It was like cheese. In the evening when my father milked the sheep, he said to me, "This sheep here, Rinio, does not have milk." And I answered him, "It didn't graze, Father." But I had milked her; I had drunk the milk. From our hunger, we didn't know what to do.

Hunger! Hunger! When we herded, we danced to entertain our hunger. Then we spread out in the fields and, without washing them, ate the greens that were not bitter. "Who will find the most greens to eat?" I grazed like a sheep, and in the evening my mouth was black from the greens I had eaten.

My childhood years we lived hidden from God. I was fifteen years old and I didn't have shoes. And my clothes were one patch on top of another. And when I saw meat, nausea gripped me. But those years were the best years because many children gathered. We herded, we danced, and we said, "Whoever dances in front and loses step will herd the sheep until evening." But I was a dancing girl, and I didn't lose my step, do you understand?

■

Whenever I went away from Elika, Irini always spoke the same farewell. "I may go traveling before you return." I wondered whether I might feel lost without her until one time, at parting, her words—like the North Star—pointed the way. "After I leave," she said, "come sit by my grave and we will talk." "Yes," I chimed in, "we'll tell stories." "And sing," Irini chuckled.

good news

"My father arrived at the house. I was in the salon sewing. He said something in a whisper to my mother. '*Po po*, you did that! Did you ask Rinio?' she said. 'Listen to you!' he replied. 'Why should I ask her? Whatever I want, I will do.' 'Good,' she replied sarcastically. 'We're going to have trouble.'

"Afterwards my mother summoned me and told me 'Rinio, your father committed an absurdity.' 'What?' I say. 'He went and arranged it with that Kambiti [a man from Kambos, a village near Neapolis]. 'With whom did he arrange it?' I ask. 'With you,' she answers.

"Later I say to my father, 'Did I ask you for marriage? No! Well, then, it's impossible!' I tell him. 'I will kill you,' he says. 'I would prefer that you kill me,' I told him. My mother, ill-fated one, cried. My father said, 'Old Woman, I will not take back my word!' I said, 'You marry him, then!' He said, 'Rather than take back my word, I would prefer to kill you.' 'Willingly,' I told him. 'Kill me. Then my girlfriends won't be able to mock me.' The Kambiti was fifteen years older than me; he was a fisherman. I didn't want him at all.

"Many wanted me, but I didn't want any of them. I wasn't very beautiful, but they had spoken for me from Kalivia and from Sparti and from Neapolis and from Yithion. I wanted to go to Yithion because I had heard that the city was heaven—not like the villages where we worked like oxen. But my parents didn't want it. I told my father, 'You didn't want to send me to Yithion, and now I don't want marriage.' I was still young; I was twenty-two. But my father had gotten old, and he said, 'I have gotten old, and I don't want to die and leave you unmarried.'

"So my father arranged it with the Kambiti. When they came to measure for the engagement ring and shoes, I didn't give them my foot—they measured my shoe. I ate wood; I took a beating. I told my father, 'The blame is on your neck if I don't live happily.' He told me, 'He is a peaceful man. You will live happily.' I told him, 'You have my word, if I'm not happy—whether you are living or dead—I will curse you all my years.' In the end, I married him for proof. And indeed Vangelis [Good News] was a saintly man.

"Vangelis was good. He never said a bad word to me. He never complained. He never slapped the children. When I slapped them, he begged that my mother's soul be forgiven. One time we were sitting on our terrace and I was looking at him. He stared at me. I said to him, 'Why are you looking at me, Vangelis? I'm pretty. That's why you're looking at me.' 'Ach, Poor One, I'm looking at you because by and by we must part.' He was so good, when he died, the stones were crying.

"There were ten children in Vangelis' family. There were seven brothers, and they had two caiques. From age twelve, Vangelis traveled by caique to Kalamata, Kriti [Crete]. He traded fish. He returned after five or six months. While he was away, I wrestled by myself. I carried sacks of olives from the fields on my back—I didn't have an animal. In the same way I carried firewood. I reaped wheat. I planted a garden—table foods.

"After we had been married one year, Vangelis stopped traveling with the caique. We built our house, and then he traded locally. He had a horse, and he transported either oil or oranges from Elika to Neapolis. From Neapolis he carried back fish and sold them—and peanuts. Our meat safe always contained fish—because of this I loathe fish now. We had everything good with Vangelis. Whatever he found in front of him, he brought us: innards, meat, cheese. In the evening when he arrived, the children searched his four pockets—two on each side—to see what was in them: roasted chickpeas, candies, sausages, cookies. 'Leave him. He's tired,' I admonished.

"Some days Vangelis went to work selling fish, and other days we went together to the field. In the beginning, not one green did he know how to tend, but little by little he learned. One week I teamed the donkeys—when I was a girl I teamed my father's donkeys, and I plowed because my father was old and couldn't work. I teamed the donkeys, and Vangelis began to plow. Gradually he learned, and I followed along behind to sow, to pick up some stones. I wanted to be with him because I felt sorry for him. He was alone; he didn't have any boys to help him. I bore six children—five girls in a row. The third girl died—Kristina, named for my mother. And the last one—a boy—was born dead.

"I raised four girls, and my old man, ill-fated one, he said, 'Don't be bitter, Rinio.' I said, 'I'm not bitter.' But there was poverty then and they asked for dowries. I was fortunate and they didn't ask me. When my daughters grew up, people told me, 'The devil will take them. Papouliena, you have the most beautiful girls.' In that way, I did not become embittered.

"But as soon as Vangelis had field work, I had to go too. I said, 'The girls will put the house in order, and I will go with their father.' Matina, my youngest, said, 'Other mothers don't leave their daughters without washing dishes or cooking or baking.' My Stavroula, the oldest, went to the fourth grade, and afterwards I left her at home for twenty days and went to Elos and picked cotton. I went three times. They paid me with cotton and, when I returned, I made quilts. Stavroula watched her father, baked bread, washed, looked after the small children. They began at a very young age and, with the help of God, the four became very good housekeepers.

"My daughters all married. First Stavroula married, Florentia second, Eleni third, and fourth Matina. I am pleased by my daughters; they have my blessing a thousand times. And I am pleased by my sons-in-law and by my grandchildren. Eleni's daughter Vangelio is like Vangelis; she resembles her grandfather."

the astronomer

Irini was known as "the Astronomer" because she was an observer and a philosopher. "I put my tail everywhere. Where I wasn't sown, I sprang up." In keeping with her reputation, Irini would like to return to Elika one hundred years after her death. She has already experienced nearly a century of change in the village where she was born, grew, married, aged, and—before long—will die. From her perspective, life in Elika now is one hundred times better than it was in her day. "I wish I were fifteen years old, not ninety as I am," she asserts.

"Life now is comfortable; people have all their conveniences. They have water at the house, and light. We didn't have either. Every morning when we got up, whether it was raining or not, we had to take jugs and go to the spring. We walked half an hour carrying the jugs on our shoulders. Now they open the faucet. They don't tire themselves, but the old days were tiring.

"Once a month we gathered our clothes to wash. My sister and I washed at the ravine. We used beautiful homemade soap my mother made—I make it now—and we beat the clothes with a wooden bat. When they were clean, we threw the clothes in the river and rinsed them. If we had time, we spread the wash out on branches to dry, but sometimes rain caught us, and we carried the clothes—half washed—back to the house. Life was a martyrdom then.

"Now they have their washing machines, and their refrigerators are full, and still some say, 'What life is this?' 'You have the monk's rabies,' I tell them. 'You should have lived my life.' I saw three wars—occupation, hunger, terror. We ran from the Italians who hunted us with guns; we hid in caves for a month without water to drink. I had four daughters, and I wove one hundred twenty lengths of fabric to make their dowries. Sometimes the oil from the lamp ran over and spotted the cloth. My husband Vangelis said to me, 'You give alms, my Rinio. Come and sleep a little bit.' Now truck vendors bring the dowry ready-made to their doors, and they buy it: blankets, clothing, undergarments, sheets. 'Whatever you want,' I tell them, 'you only have to have money, and you have money.'

"Now they earn thousand-drachma notes, and they don't know where to put all their things. Whoever had a thousand-drachma note in my day was the richest person in the village. I had to clear bushes for ten days to collect ten drachmas. I had nothing when I married. One day I bought a knife. The next day, a fork. Give my regards to poverty!

"Money didn't exist in my day. After I married, I went to the *apalaitika* with my sisters and cousins—sometimes five women, sometimes ten all together. Today we go to my fields, tomorrow to yours. We reaped wheat, we gathered olives, we weeded seedlings. Some sang, others danced, we laughed—we were great company. And we had a lot of work. What we knew how to do, we did. Now they don't weed; they don't reap. They have herbicides and machines. The machines reap and thresh and bale the wheat, and someone oversees the machine. There is no companionship, and without companionship, you don't sing, you don't laugh, you don't say anything. It isn't good.

"They want a better life now, but they don't understand how to better their lives. Love, peace, good family relations—this is joy. And if they want money, they can have it. They can spend it on their children, but not to have vagabonds who come and go and girls who get pregnant. The parents are responsible for their children, but they leave them too independent and they give them a lot of money. Money spoils people. They become greedy. They want to have everything they see, and when one has and another doesn't, the one complains, 'Why should you have a car, and I don't have one?' And the other one brags, 'I am better than you.'

"One day the neighbor women were talking, and I said, 'What does it matter if Tsigounis' wife wears an expensive dress and I don't? It doesn't concern me how much she paid for it—let her pay five or six thousand drachmas. But when I don't have one drachma, why should I have such a dress? If she has grace and if she has respect, does anything else matter? Don't I speak the truth?' I have heard the women say, 'What a beautiful dress Zoe is wearing.' And I tell them, 'She deserves it, and a better one still.'"

homing

Wanting to sink my roots deep into bedrock, I asked Mihail to take me to Skopeles. Skopeles is a region three kilometers north of Elika. Several generations before Elika's founding, shepherds built their *kalivia* in this valley, which was invisible to pirates who cruised the gulf and pillaged coastal settlements. The Turks destroyed Skopeles, Mihail informed me, forty or fifty years before the War of Independence, which began in 1821. The earth long ago reclaimed building stone and mortar mud. The foundation of one lone chapel, like a giant tombstone, marks Skopeles' community grave.

At the time appointed for our excursion, I met Mihail at the telephone *cafenio*. He was talking to a man named Yiorgos who, like numerous other villagers, has returned from Athina to Elika for retirement. Yiorgos owns neither saddle horse nor motorized vehicle, so when he heard our destination he asked to join us. He has trees in the neighborhood of Skopeles, and he wanted to look them over.

The three of us climbed into Mihail's maroon Jeep, which powered us up a mountain road to the chapel Panayia, the

"Virgin Mary." There, instead of turning right toward Andonis and Martha's *kalivi* at Siamenes, we headed left toward Skopeles where the young Irini, in the tradition of Skopeles' ill-fated inhabitants, herded for a living.

When we reached Skopeles, we got out of the Jeep and walked a few steps to the foundation of Ay Stefanos—an assemblage of stones as resistant to winter deluge as the surrounding vegetation is impervious to summer drought. The unusual curved outline of the chapel raised more questions than could be answered.

From Ay Stefanos we walked a few meters to a modern chapel called Zoodhohos Pigi, the "Life-Giving Fountain"— another name for the Virgin Mary. Villagers congregate at the chapel only once a year, on the Friday after Easter. The chapel doors were unlocked, and we entered. As I looked about, Yiorgos told a story brought to mind by a large horizontally fluted clay olive oil jar standing in the corner by the door.

Every year, Yiorgos told me, the parishioners fill the jar with oil to light the votive lamps in the chapel. One time the parishioners noticed that the oil level was dropping unusually quickly, and they suspected that someone was stealing oil. To find out, one villager hid in the sanctum and waited. Eventually a man from Elika came into the chapel, crossed himself, and stood in front of the ikon of the Virgin Mary, the same ikon Yiorgos had kissed when he entered the chapel.

The thief pleaded his case to the Virgin. "I am a poor man from Elika, and I have a large number of children. No matter how hard I work, it seems there is never enough food for my family. Virgin Mary, I beseech you, may I have some oil for my children?"

In an attempt to intimidate the thief, the parishioner hiding behind the ikon of Christ thundered, "No!" "I'm not asking you. I'm asking your mother," the thief retorted.

When we left the chapel, Mihail, Yiorgos, and I gravitated toward a massive olive tree anchored nearby. I sat on a rock under the tree that had also shaded the shepherds of Skopeles and, perhaps, their executioners. And I recalled the story Mihail had once told me about the ancestral village.

■

In the days of the Turkish occupation, the bey or local governor lived in Monemvasia. Periodically he sent a representative to collect taxes from the villages in his province. The tax collector traveled by animal. One time the collector rented a mule belonging to a man from Lira, a village high on the mountain above Skopeles. The owner, a fellow named Steloyiorgos, walked behind the collector, who rode the mule.

This tax collector had offended Steloyiorgos by flirting with his beautiful wife. When the pair reached a secluded spot, Steloyiorgos took out a pistol and shot the man to death. He hid the body in the bush. Before the tax collector was missed, a shepherd herding in the area noticed a peculiar smell and a restlessness in his flock. He looked and found the corpse, which he reported to the Turkish authorities. The authorities questioned Steloyiorgos, who said bandits had ambushed and killed the tax collector and that he himself had been released unharmed.

Wanting to retaliate, the bey requested soldiers from the higher authorities in Tripolis. When a cavalry company arrived, the bey sent it to Skopeles, the village closest to the spot where the body was found. The soldiers incinerated the village and murdered everyone but the young people, who were taken to Tripolis to be enslaved.

En route to Tripolis, one boy tried to persuade a girl to attempt an escape with him. The girl was fearful and refused. But when the company traversed a particularly rough and wooded area, the boy did escape. That boy, named Simiyiannis, eventually settled and raised a family in Dhemonia, the first village north of Elika on the main road. This Simiyiannis was the only survivor of the holocaust at Skopeles, and his successors are the only descendants of Elika's ancestral village.

■

The current of history carried me deep into Skopeles' past. I lingered there until a man's voice snapped me back to the present. Yiorgos, standing a few paces away from me in the shade of the same ancient olive, was recounting a more recent chapter in Skopeles' history. Forty years ago, before Elikans started going to Marathia to garden and swim during July and August, ten families roped their *kotetsia* to their packsaddles and resettled in Skopeles' more temperate mountain climate for the summer. They subsisted on produce from gardens irrigated by spring water, and they took shelter in stone huts not unlike the *kalivia* the original settlers had built.

I don't know how their ancestral village has affected people from Elika, but Skopeles has possessed me. Is it today's beguiling cypresses rising decisively from hill-sides ribbed with stone walls, and the emerald-leafed *platana* trees suckling underground springs? Or is it a yearning to complete a long-ago-interrupted flight—a need to sing a song I had but half sung?

interior landscape

Voula

Yiorgos

Theodhori's flock

reaping

roofing the *mantri*

boy pulling onions

the goatherd Martha

Martha in her *kalivi*

autumn sun

Elika

"master craftsman" at work

gathering olives

carrying fodder

horsepower

Spiros scribing the earth

spiral mountain

"Let's go to the Alikioti," the men would say. Alikioti is a man from Alika, a village on the western tip of the Mani. But this particular Alikioti no longer lived in the Mani. Sometime within a decade or two after 1827 when the Greeks ousted the Turks, he left Alika, perhaps to find more arable land elsewhere, perhaps to avoid a vendetta against him, perhaps because he was wanted for a criminal offense. He crossed the Lakonian Gulf and, halfway up the western coast, within view of the Mani in fair weather, he founded a new village along with other Maniotes, shepherds, and emigres from British-dominated Kythira. Over time, "Let's go to the Alikioti" became "Let's go to the Elikioti." The man was so popular, the new village assumed his name—or so one story goes.

Mihail has long doubted that Elika derived her name from another place name. Traditionally administrators have assigned the names of towns and villages in Greece. Because of this, Mihail reasons that the name Elika was chosen because of its inherent meaning, "helix" or "spiral." This notion tortured Mihail until 1990 when he stumbled upon some substantive evidence in *New Laws and Decrees of the Post-Justinian Era*, written by C. E. Zacharia Lingenthal and translated by Ioannis D. Zepos. One passage referred to ecclesiastical matters of Monemvasia's chief bishop at the time of the emperor Manuel Paleologos in the fourteenth century A.D. In particular, the emperor offered the bishop a section of land bounded on one side by the Elikovounon or "Spiral Mountain." Mihail is convinced that this Elikovounon is the mountain that wraps around Elika and "embraces her as a mother embraces her child," and he is convinced that administrators named Elika after this designation in a long-forgotten official document.

As Elika grew, neighborhoods emerged and assumed names of their own. Kokkinitsa for some reason took its name from *kokkino*, the color red. Prosiliaka, or "sunny," derives its name from the fact that when the sun rises, its rays strike that ridgetop neighborhood first.

One time Lambi described my house as *prosiliako*, but my house is located on the opposite side of the village in one of Elika's oldest neighborhoods called Maravelianika. The name is taken from Maravelias, the predominant surname in the neighborhood. Surnames have tended to cluster in the village because a bride traditionally went to live in a house her husband provided—either his father's house or a house built on a subdivision of his father's estate. The neighborhood Kousoulianika is named after the surname Kousoulis, and Hadhiarianika is derived from the surname Hadhiaris. The name of Elika's other neighborhood, Stratianika, comes from the masculine-gender first name, Stratis.

Surnames in Greek are imbued with geographic and sociological meaning. The name endings indicate the family's place of origin. The suffix -*akos*, as in Kaloyerakos, places the origin in the Mani. The suffix -*akis* indicates a background in Kriti—for example, Yiannarakis, the name of a taxi driver in Elika.

The root of a surname indicates the profession or character of the ancestor. *Papas* means "priest." The Papadhakis brothers trace their heritage to a priest in Kriti. The descendants of a priest in the Mani are called Papadhakos, and those from the Peloponnese outside Lakonia, Papadhopoulos.

Mihail Tsigounis' family came via Kythira from Epiros in northern Greece, and his surname immortalizes a characteristic of his great-great-great-grandfather. According to legend, this man asked a tailor to cut a vest from a length of woolen cloth probably woven by his wife. The piece was skimpy for the vest he wanted, but rather than supply a larger piece of cloth, the man told the tailor to economize and cut the vest anyway. From this event, the family acquired a name meaning "stingy."

I once interviewed an elderly widower named Kousoulis who told me, "First of all, for a woman to be good to her husband, she must be moral. And after that, she must esteem her father-in-law and her mother-in-law more than her own parents." Consistent with the patriarchy, once a woman married, she was known outside the family by a variation of her husband's surname. Beligrena is Belagrakos' wife. The wife of Papadhakis is called Papadhakena. Thea is sometimes called Monolitsena.

Sometimes a wife is known by her husband's first name. Hence Thea is also called Monolou. Mihail's grandmother Eleni was called Mihaliakena, and his mother Yioryia was known as Theodhorikena. Zoe might have been called Mihalou, but like most younger wives in Elika, she has chosen to be addressed by her own name.

The value placed on the paternal side of the family is also reflected in the system by which children are named—a system that both simplifies and complicates identifying individuals. The first son is usually named for his paternal grandfather, while the first daughter is given the name of her paternal grandmother. The second son and daughter take the names of their maternal grandparents.

Because of this pattern, one can usually determine the grandparents' names from the grandchildren's names and vice versa. But when a man has several sons, each of whom names a son after his paternal grandfather, the first cousins must be identified by their father's first name. In Elika, a Lambi Houlis fathered three sons, who each fathered a first son named Lambi Houlis. The man from whom I purchased my house is Lambi Houlis of Dhimitris. Little Soula's father, who runs the telephone *cafenio*, is Lambi Houlis of Yiannis. The third first cousin, who lives near my first rental, is Lambi Houlis of Yiorgos.

Exceptions to the naming system are made. The father of the Lambi from Ay Mammas, for whom I picked olives, was a sickly infant. His mother believed that by baptizing him Efstratios in Maravelianika's chapel Ay Stratigos, he would heal. Stratis did heal; he does not bear his paternal grandfather's name.

In other cases a child is named after a beloved relative who has died. For example, a widower who remarries may name his first daughter by his second wife after his first wife. Sometimes too a daughter is named after a grandfather, or a son after a grandmother. This is possible because many Greek names have a masculine and a feminine form: Panayiotis/ Panayiota, Paraskevas/Paraskevi, Vasilis/Vasilia. Knowing this led me to think Irini's granddaughter was named after Irini's husband Vangelis, but in fact she was given the name of her paternal grandmother, Vangelia. Today families tend to have two children; the first may be named after a paternal grandparent and the second after a maternal grandparent.

A family traditionally was free to select any name for the third and subsequent sons and daughters. Often the third son or daughter is named for the village guardian saint. Elika's saint is Ay Haralambos, a priest who died in Asia Minor at age one hundred thirteen. He died in martyrdom; he was skinned alive by the Romans. His skeleton was delivered to the island Evia and, according to custom, small parts of it have been distributed to many villages across Greece. Their churches are named for their patron saint, and they celebrate his day on February tenth, the day he died and gave his soul to God.

Because Haralambos is Elika's saint's name, Haralambos is the most common man's name in the village. Yiorgos, Stratis, Mihalis, and Panayiotis are also popular. The most common women's names are Matina, Eleni, and Kriso, along with Maria, Yioryia, and Panayiota. To help distinguish and personalize individuals with the same name, names are often abbreviated or given a diminutive form, or both. Haralambos is usually shortened to Lambi or to the diminutive Lambrakis. Mitsos and Mimi are short forms of Dhimitris. Panayotis is often shortened to Taki. Efstratios becomes Stratis or Stratos.

Similarly, Eleni may become Elenitsa; Kaliopi, Kaliopitsa; Yioryia, Yitsa; Potula, Potitsa. Kriso may become Krisoula, which is often clipped to Soula. Evangelia may be known as Vangelia or Vangelio, or as Angella, which may be diminutized to Angeliki and Angeliko. Fotini becomes Fotinoula or Fofoula. Voula derives from Stavroula or from Paraskevoula, the diminutive of Paraskevi.

With the advent of the pickup truck, villagers began to distinguish men with the same name by the colors of their vehicles. With the large number of trucks in Elika today, this approach may be losing its effectiveness.

The redundancy of names in Elika has complicated my journal-keeping, especially because I rarely know last names. My solution is to use notations based on spouse, parent, role, or some other detail which only I can decipher. Take Lambi. I refer to Lambi/house, Lambi/cafe, Lambi/truck, Lambi/big truck, Lambi/baker, Lambi/trash, Lambi/corner house, Lambi/Stratis, Lambi/Kristofili, Lambi/Nikos, Lambi/Theodhoris, Lambi/Eleni. Or Matina: Matina/shepherd, Matina/blue eyes, Matina/Pericles, Matina/Belagrakos, Matina/Vangelis, Matina/Spiros, Matina/3 kids.

I am always grateful when someone has a name I cannot confuse. I know only one Ksanthi, one Liyeri, one Potula, and one Theodhosis in Elika.

I am moved by the beauty of the Greek names, which often derive from archaic names—Pericles, Aphrodite—or the names of saints. At the same time, I wonder how names affect their bearers. Garifalia means "carnation," Kanellia means "cinnamon," Zoe is "life," Eleftheria is "freedom," Sophia is "wisdom," and Irini is "peace." Kyriaki means "Sunday," Stavroula derives from "cross," and Fani is short for Theofania, or "appearance of God."

I came to Elika in 1974 as Mary, which easily became

Maria. In 1980 I legally changed my given name Mary Ann to Thordis. I wanted a Norwegian first name to complement my surname, because I am the last Simonsen in my father's lineage, and I would never relinquish the family name. I adopted a first name a friend suggested that belonged to a vigorous old Norwegian woman my friend once met.

I understand now that giving up the name my mother chose for me was a bold statement of independence—my mother's name is Marian, her mother's name was Marian, my sister's name is Ann, and I had several close friends named Mary at the time.

In the States even my mother honors my name Thordis. The situation is different in Elika. People who bestow their parents' names on their children don't easily understand why I would give up my mother's name. And Thordis, though I pronounce the *h* in Greece, is difficult for the villagers to master. In fact, some villagers enjoy confusing my name with the Greek word *pordhi*, "fart." Some villagers call me by my name, some still simply refer to me as "the American," others persist in calling me Maria, and some address me by the Greek name that comes closest to Thordis—Theodhora, meaning "gift of God." My own name means "Thor's sprite" or "messenger"—Thor is the Nordic thunder god. When I chose the name Thordis, I had no idea that my way station would be located on the side of the Spiral Mountain.

elika

My favorite route into Elika begins at Kefalies, where the roads from Siamenes and Skopeles, farther up, converge. In the fall when purple heather sanctifies the land, I hike these mountain precincts to pick wild *koumara* and to forage wild greens—just as my ninety-eight-year-old *yiayia* did in her childhood. In the spring when the perfume of golden broom hangs heavy in the air like incense, I look for my friend Theodhoris and his flock. No matter what the nature of my upland excursion, the return passage through the junction, with the sudden first reappearance of Elika and the sea, is the crowning glory. If the return is made at sunset or under a full moon, all the more reason to celebrate.

The road down into Elika from the junction follows the contours of the hillsides. Again the village disappears. The road declines steeply. Finally it levels off at a boulder on the left—part of an old *mantri* built into a sheer rock facade. Shadows of passing midwives and matchmakers have swept across the face of the boulder. Children and perhaps armed rebels have climbed or hidden behind it. The boulder has seen tractors and trucks come and mules and oxen go. This megalith is my gatepost into Elika.

A few paces beyond and to the right is Vangelis Hadhiaris' house. Like the back of a broken donkey, the tile roof of this two-room dwelling sags under the weight of the demands long made of it. Vangelis Hadhiaris raised the original slate and earthen roof himself. In one tiny room with its low narrow doorway and corner hearth, the roof sheltered Vangelis, his wife, and their children. They cooked and ate in this room, and then they unrolled rush mats and the entire family slept together on the earthen floor. While those his wife had already borne slept, Vangelis sired more children—seven boys and one girl in all. The second equally tiny room with its own doorway and hearth served as a stable.

Vangelis' fifth child was Andonis, the shepherd. Andonis married and raised his three children in his father's house. In 1954 at age eighteen, Andonis' middle child and only son, Vangelis, began to build a small one-room house adjacent to his grandfather's. For two years Vangelis quarried building stone in the mountains. When they passed the rock megalith, his two donkeys knew they had reached home with one more load of stone.

For two more years, Vangelis set stones in mud mortar. In 1972 at age thirty-six, this Vangelis married. For eighteen years his wife Matina cooked in the kitchen of his grandfather's house, and he, Matina, and their two children slept on beds in the house Vangelis built.

In 1985 Vangelis began to build another house—this one a two-story four-room concrete and brick structure paid for with drachmas amassed from the sale of olive oil and onions. Before the family moved into the centrally located new house in 1989, Matina explained, their children were isolated in the old neighborhood, and the old house was too long a walk from the school bus, especially in rainy weather. After she had lived in the more spacious new house for a year, she commented that it was a more loving life when children had less space and fewer things, which they shared equally.

In the fall of 1990, in preparation for the 1991 census, a number was assigned to each of the three hundred fifty-nine houses in Elika. I'm not sure what constitutes a house. The two-house complex built by Vangelis and his grandfather received one number: 157. Other vacated but habitable dwellings were left unnumbered. My own house was not numbered during the last census a decade ago when the structure functioned as a *mantri*, but the new roof built in 1990 restored the structure to house status. The *"mantri"* was assigned the number 359.

The houses in Elika represent a medley of architectural styles. Over a century old, my own simple stone dwelling is one of Elika's original houses. During restoration, I have attempted to preserve its natural character; I even replaced the hand-carved wooden-lidded pitcher that had been built into the kitchen wall as a receptacle for forks and knives.

Over the years the villagers have awkwardly enlarged and modernized their old family homes, or they have built entirely new ones—Vangelis has done so twice! As a result of these creations and transformations, one finds sleek plastic and aluminum closures installed alongside hand-milled wooden windows and doors, geometric cinderblock walls and wire fences extending richly textured stone walls and brush fences, and prefabricated chimney stacks poking up among those improvised from ridged terra cotta storage jars.

Numerous *kotetsia* and goat stalls also display the villagers' facility for vernacular architecture. I will always savor the memory of a blossoming-oleander-branch roof that graced a *kotetsi* one summer. And I marvel at the assemblage of discarded wooden window shutters and doors—fifteen in all—that form the walls of a goat shed near the old Ay Haralambos church.

Although I've only seen one flower-bedecked *kotetsi* in Elika, carnations, roses, geraniums, bougainvillea, and honeysuckle adorn most houses. And in addition to garden mint and rosemary, at least one potted basil plant sits on most stairways. I will always remember Dhespina, who at age eleven brought me my first potted basil.

Although villagers do most of their retail shopping in Neapolis, Elika supports a small number of shops. Papadhakis Brothers *bakaliko/taverna*—with its rotund wine casks, marble-topped tables, and shelves stocked with condensed milk and motor oil—was established in 1950. Yiorgos Hadhiaris, a cousin to Vangelis' children, opened his bakery next door to Papadhakis Brothers in 1990. At that time Elika supported two *bakalika*, three *cafenia*, two *taverna/* restaurants, two butcher shops, two video game cafeteria/ bars, a gasoline station, an auto repair shop, an auto body shop, an electrician's shop, and a metalsmith's shop. A small supermarket and a carpentry shop were preparing to open. Most of these commercial establishments are located on a road that curves like a horseshoe up from the main road and around the new Ay Haralambos cathedral, completed in 1950 with the help of Greek-American money. All houses in Elika are within easy walking distance of any of the shops.

At night in the summertime, cousins and grandkids vacationing from Athina and abroad give the streets in Elika a carnival-like atmosphere. At other times, Elika reclaims her theater-like intimacy. Widows dressed in black head scarves and dresses perch on low walls where they crochet and socialize to pass the time. On dewy winter mornings an occasional horse, bearing a rider and a long ladder, clops along the street en route to the olive grove. And year round, truck vendors—like walk-ons—hawk fish, "aromatic apples," and "plastic ware for every kitchen, for every household."

Elika refers to herself as a geriatric village because so few youth choose to make Elika their home. Some Elikans also say the villagers are not good people. "When they see you prosper they gossip, and one will mock the other." I have seen villagers laugh at a neighbor woman who suffered periods of hysteria. But I also see the women share the responsibility of round-the-clock nursing for the dying and volunteer hours preparing *kourambiedhes* in a hot bakery for Yiorgos' opening celebration.

And I feel the power of Elika's communal love when villagers congregate at the church to bid one of their own a final farewell, and when the old men sitting outside Papadhakis Brothers *bakaliko/taverna* rise and extend their hands to wish the American girl, after a long absence from the village, a "good arrival."

good road, good life

"Are you married?" they ask me.

One time I boarded the bus ahead of the other passengers from Neapolis. Although she had forty-nine vacant seats to choose from, the next passenger to board plunked herself down in the seat beside me—a stranger and a foreigner to boot. Another time I was seated on a more crowded bus from Athina. As soon as a woman settled down beside me, she faced me and asked, "Where is your other?" I looked at her. "Are you alone?" she pursued.

"Why don't you marry?" they ask me.

One time I was visiting Irini's daughter Eleni, who held her sixteen-month-old grandnephew Stathis in her lap. She helped him turn a green circular plastic dish, which steered an imaginary car. "Vroom, vroom, vroom"—Eleni taught him to drive fast. Four years later, Stathis' two-year-old sister Florentia was playing in her grandparents' small enclosed garden. When she climbed one step up from the ground onto a retaining wall, her mother called, "Get down! You'll fall! Where is your doll?"

"You must marry!" they insist.

One time I asked Thea what people used to say about girls who did not marry. "'An old maid,' they said, 'stays on the shelf. We put her there where we set bottles.' It was difficult then," Thea explained. "The young men looked at the pretty ones and the young in age. If a girl passed twenty-five years and went toward thirty, they didn't want her. The family said, 'What will become of this girl now? Wherever we go they indict her—she takes the bad road.'" When I asked Thea what happened to spinsters, she told me they became servants to their married brothers and raised their children.

■

In Greece, companionship is highly valued; many boys and girls continue to be taught traditional gender roles; and the unmarried daughter traditionally has been an embarrassment to her family. No wonder almost everyone I encounter eventually inquires about my marital status. Very few tell me it is better to be single. Most admonish me to marry. Now they even tell me I have a dowry—my house.

"We'll see," I reply. I grew up and went through college thinking I would marry; I didn't know I had an alternative. But I never wanted marriage with the certainty and immediacy that I wanted to teach or wanted to write. I didn't picture myself married the way I have pictured my restored house in

Elika. But I remained open to the possibility of marriage "down the road" until my soul ventured aloft while I wrote "Flying the Horizon." When I read the words I had scribed, I knew indeed I would not marry. Then I began to tell the villagers, "No, I travel another road," or "No, I listen to a different voice."

It has not been easy to claim my womanhood in a culture that equates womanhood with marriage—a single woman is a *yerontokori*, an "old girl." I look much younger than most of my women contemporaries in Elika. My blond hair camouflages my prized gray ones. I have a small frame and am lanky; by nature I do not carry the bulk of most mature Greek women. And unlike theirs, my skin is fair and unweathered. I sense that if more villagers knew I am the same age as Ksanthi—who has two grown sons—they would be even more alarmed by my independence. Instead, they simply call me *koritsi*—"little girl"—and continue to wave a stick at me.

I appreciate the villagers' good intentions and only feel roused when someone tells me, "Yours is not a good life." I think about all the women in Elika who raise their children and manage the land single-handedly while their husbands earn a living traveling for the better part of the year in the merchant marine. And I think about all the widowed women who have lived alone—Kaliopi for sixty years—because remarriage for women has been proscribed. And I simply state, "I'm glad if your life is good for you; my life is good for me."

I recognize how life in Elika puts my choices to the test. I only become angry when a man assumes, because I am not married, that I am an object for his consumption. None of the men in Elika has ever treated me degradingly. But when I am hitchhiking locally, sometimes a man I don't know gives me a ride, and when he starts fidgeting and asking questions that are too personal, I wish the local buses ran at more convenient hours, and I chastise myself for not lying more easily. I could have said I was married—before he asked!

The villagers do not ask whether I have children, but when they proclaim the necessity of marriage, they imply the virtue of motherhood. Yiorgos Papadhakis revealed this to me when he said, "It's all right to be free now when you are young, but if you don't have children, who will help you when you are old?" Yiorgos has a son in Patras, a son in Thessaloniki, and a daughter in Athina. You are aging, Yiorgos, I observe to myself. Where are your children?

The fact is, until I acknowledged and healed my own "inner child" in psychotherapy during my late thirties and early forties, I was not inclined toward motherhood. By the time the urge awakened, I was too committed to a different life and knew so. I grieved the children I never bore. Later, when I saw that the chimney I built at my house suggested a pregnant woman's torso, I realized I had come to terms with my choice—or destiny.

Happily, children have come into my life in Elika at the same time that my *yiayia* Irini prepares to go traveling. Matina, the shepherd Theodhoris' daughter, greets me—as does her father—with arms open wide. When she was younger, she would grasp my hand and hold onto it while we walked together across a mountain pasture. She would look deeply perplexed one moment; the next, her face would glow like a lamp in the dark.

And Yiorgos, a teenager who, the summer I roofed my house, carried roof tiles, roof timbers, and the last truckload of sand down from the road. When I suggested he slow down, he sped up. When I urged him to carry less, he carried more. At eighteen, anything was possible, but not in Elika. He prepared to leave—if not America, the merchant marine.

And Effi, Eleni and Andonis' granddaughter who grew up in Athina but spent the summers of her childhood years in Elika. With hugs, she delivered warm *paksimadhia* and fresh *kourambiedhes* from her grandmother's oven, and she played in my house. Sweeping dust off my ladder and patting mortar meatballs, she played *nikokira*. Just as often she planted and irrigated wheat on my unpaved floors, or she stuccoed my walls with mud. Intensely free, balanced, and loving, she is the child I hope to become.

And there is Dhespina—the cherub. One summer I went to the beach on the eve of my departure from Elika for the winter. Dhespina frolicked offshore. When she saw me, she splashed her way onto the beach beside me. She picked up a driftwood stick, etched the outline of a heart in the sand, and, darting off, chirped, "Lucky I saw you!"

"Likewise!" I called after her.

this blessed house

How many times have the villagers scolded me for not sleeping during the *mesimeri?* Why did my neighbor Krisoula call to me one hot July afternoon when she could see that I had worked too late? And why did I respond to her summons rather than excuse myself and continue on my way?

"Where are you going?" Krisoula's cheerless voice emanated from a densely shaded veranda. "I have just finished working at my house. I'm tired; I'm going to my rental to nap," I explained. "Don't sleep; come sit," she implored. Wearily I pushed open the sagging wire gate, dragged past an assembly of potted basil and blooming plants, and slumped into the chair opposite her. Absent-mindedly, I plucked a sprig of spearmint from a plant creeping within reach. In long-drawn breaths, I inhaled its freshness while I inventoried her garden: lemon, pomegranate, apple, and peach trees in different phases of productivity; burgeoning zucchini, tomato, eggplant, and bean; windblown feed corn; resplendent roses; scarlet geraniums; and spent artichokes.

"Do you like it here?" Krisoula posed. Do all those who

ask me this question think I have no choice in the matter? I wondered. "Of course," I sighed. Unaffected by my passivity, she launched into an all too familiar refrain, and I listened politely. "When you finish your house, you must find someone to marry. Bring him here and stay year round." Krisoula's speech became impassioned. "You will become a *nikokira*; you will become a woman. You will have children to play at your house like we did."

"Like we did!" These words electrified me. "You played at my house?" I blurted out. "I played at your house, certainly. I was born in your house, and I played there with my brothers and sisters." Her meaning penetrated the dry soil of my consciousness. Deliberately, I interrogated her. "How long ago were you born in my house? How old are you now?" "I am seventy now; I was born in your house in 1916." Laid down, her words became footprints. They led me, like the explorer, along an unfamiliar path to an unanticipated reward.

"At the house you purchased," Krisoula began, "my mother became a bride. On her wedding night, my father became impatient. He quarreled with the guests and brandished his rifle. 'Why do you do this, Yiannis?' the guests asked. 'Because I want to drive away my in-laws so I can sleep with my bride.'

"My father was poor, and he took my mother as his wife," Krisoula confided. "She was from Ay Anargyi, a hamlet on the other side of Neapolis. My father brought her here, and since he was poor and had nothing of his own, they rented your house. It was an old house then, with a slate roof. The roof was made with beams, and they laid slates on top of the beams, and afterwards they put on earth and beat it. Later, when it rained and the earth was moist, they put on more and packed it so it would not leak.

"And the kitchen had no floor," she recalled. "It was as it is now—earthen. Only the upper room above the stable had a plank floor. That room had a shuttered, arched window, and from it we surveyed the village below. The cold came in the window, and the rain."

Seeing that I followed her story intently, Krisoula continued. "We had no furniture at all then. When we ate, we sat cross-legged on the floor at the *sofra*. All the children sat at the *sofra* and ate. And we slept on the floor—we threw down quilts and slept. And my mother bore her children on the floor. We were five children. Three of us she bore in your kitchen. She laid some stones on the earth, set herself down on them, labored, and delivered."

I first met Krisoula in 1974, ten years before I bought my house and became her neighbor. But even then she must have had some premonition about me because at the end of our first brief encounter, she promised to bequeath her house to me—she and her husband Andreas produced no heirs. She had reiterated her promise the day before our conversation. Now I understood: when I purchased my house, I inherited her birthplace, and I became the daughter she had yearned to bear. I opened my heart to Krisoula as she continued her story.

"It was dark in the house because it didn't have windows—only one, as I told you. And the walls were unplastered, as you found them. And then there was no electricity. With one oil lamp, what light does it make in a stone and earthen house?

"I was fearful when I was small and it grew dark. We cried when my mother had not returned to light the oil lamp.

Many times we cried and asked what might turn up in the roof, because we were afraid of snakes. Big snakes entered the house, and adders. They frightened us because when an adder bites you, you die, my Virgin Mary! So we went outside in the dark and cried, my two brothers and I, and many times sleep overtook us, and we slept outside on the ground. When the neighbors came by, they took us in the house and we slept there. They closed the doorway with branches and left us like animals. And they would call my mother, 'Stupid Maria, why do you leave your children alone? The snakes will bite them, and they will die.' She answered, 'What can I do, I who am poor and come and go in order to bring bread to eat!'

"We were poor. As children, we walked the roads barefoot and ragged, while the other children had their little shoes and stockings. They were privileged; we children didn't have shoes. And they ate bread and cheese, while we went hungry. We were so poor, we stole lemons and oranges and ate the rind. One time the owner seized us, and he went to my mother, and she raged, 'Why do you beat my children whilst they starve? They ate one of your lemons, and I will pay you for it so you will not thrash my children who are hungry.' And my mother wept.

"My mother worked, but my father was lazy. From morning to evening he sat at the *taverna* and drank. He came home drunk, and he whipped my mother—he beat her like a donkey. He held her and beat her a lot, and we cried. We felt sorry for my mother and when we grew, we fell on him and insulted him and he didn't beat her. My father was bad, very bad.

"But the neighbors gave us a piece of bread because they

loved my mother—she was a good woman. She did what she could by herself. Sometimes she collected olives, and she grazed sheep. She wanted to have the sheep in order to make clothes for us. She sheared the wool, spun it, and made us clothes on the loom. She made them for us so we could marry—we were three girls.

"My mother worked, and she raised us. And God protected us. He protected us, and we became grown women. My mother married us; she married us without clothes, without anything. But she gave us to good men—we all three took good men. And we worked and we made it. And we loved my mother because she was a good mother—all the children, we loved her, ill-fated one."

"And my house, what happened to my house?" I implored. "We vacated your house when I was five. We moved into the house above yours by the mulberry tree. My two sisters were born there. Your house remained unoccupied. Lambi Houlis closed sheep inside. It was a *mantri*."

I recalled the history Lambi had related to me earlier. More than one hundred years ago, my house belonged to Polychronis Maravelias. He was married to a woman whose name, Kalomira, means "fortunate one." Ironically, she died giving birth to their third child, a daughter named Kalomira in her memory. Polychronis was killed—I didn't learn how. After the three daughters married and left, my house remained deserted except for the five years when Krisoula and her family lived there. At some time Lambi inherited the house from Dhimitris Maravelias, his maternal grandfather. Because he had no use for the roofless ruin—except as a *mantri*—he sold the house to me.

Krisoula's narrative completed the history of my house

that Lambi had begun to reconstruct. It also revealed an impoverished beginning that had bloomed into a magnanimous spirit—Krisoula, who welcomes me as her daughter and would have me take her hard-earned garden, house, and belongings save the glass from which she drinks water.

But the blessing Krisoula bestowed on my house that day will always be her greatest gift to me. "How do you feel about my fixing your house?" I asked. "I like it," she beamed. "I tell people, 'An American girl bought it and fixes it by herself. She gives life to this house again. It will give light.'"

elikiotissa

When I went to Elika for the first time in 1974, piped water and electricity and pavement had already arrived, but agriculture still ran primarily on human and animal power, and people still communicated face to face. Since 1974 sporty red sedans and household telephones have appeared along with new attitudes and modes of expression. Elika is reaching, experimenting, discovering, ripening.

During these same sixteen years I have undergone my own unpremeditated metamorphosis. I have become, I am told, a woman of Elika—an Elikiotissa.

I crisscrossed every part of Elika during my trip to the village in the summer of 1974. Villagers seeing me for the first time stared, and children made a game of touching me with their fingertips. Before long, I became a familiar sight, and women vied for my presence at their dinner tables. Little Soula, my five-year-old neighbor, became my constant companion and ducked whenever possible in front of my camera. I was called "the Tourista." I observed the village "scene." I recorded what I viewed on film and in my journal.

When I went back to Elika in the summer of 1981, the villagers I had known greeted me with thanks for the photographs I had sent them and by which they had remembered me. They welcomed my return; it verified my response to the question they all had asked me in 1974: do you like it here? My answer had always been an emphatic "Yes!"

The summer of 1981, I became known as "the Teacher." I was invited to weddings and pig slaughters as well as meals, but I continued to play the role of observer until the eve of my departure. On my last walk through the village, I encountered an older woman, widowed and dressed in black, who ferried golden bundles of hay across her yard to winter storage. Rather than interrupt her work to provide hospitality for the American guest, she accepted my offer to help. I had become, at last, a participant.

Beginning in the fall of 1982, I lived in Elika for two consecutive years. In keeping with my intent to document village life in narratives and on film, I interviewed key villagers with the help of translators and made photographs. But I also participated in village life, not only to validate my observations, but to test, through personal experience, the values I had adopted while teaching, during the past eight years, an anthropology course I had designed. I went to sea with the fishermen, I picked olives, I cut onions, I weeded garlic.

One day I sat and talked with an itinerant saddlemaker who worked in the shade of a grape arbor, but within sight of prospective customers passing by. He replaced—probably for the last time—the padding on a few well-used packsaddles. When one villager happened by, the saddlemaker called out, "She tells me she has lived in Elika for over a year now." The other man proclaimed, "Yes, it's true. She's an Elikiotissa now!"

I was elated—a woman of Elika! But who is the woman of Elika? How does she live?

She marries. Thereafter, for a lifetime, she spends very little time in bed. On baking days she rises in the night and kneads her dough by lamplight. On washing days she may pin clothes on the line by moonlight.

I went to Elika with a desire to experience the village woman's life first hand. I established a household of my own where, like the *nikokira*, I cook and wash and clean and sew. On some days I work in the olive groves or the onion fields. The villagers respect my hard work, and they reciprocate my love. They regard me as an insider.

But I also live alone, read, write, and make photographs. I have no children of my own. And when there is "men's work" to do, I do it without hesitating. My lifestyle puzzles the women, who embrace me but at the same time regard me as an outsider.

My dual status in Elika carries with it certain privileges. My neighbor Matina revealed her deepest sorrow to me, but she beseeched me not to tell the other villagers. Ironically, she shared her confidence because of our differences, whereas the feelings she expressed illuminate our similarities.

This anecdote suggests why the villagers call me an Elikiotissa. What the women of Elika and I share is not something tangible and measurable. What we have in common are feelings that need to be expressed and a human spirit that wants to be set free.

Martha the goatherd, my sidekick Thea, and my soulmate Irini disowned the yoke of village tradition. Unhobbled, Martha travels the highlands with her goats. Taking the plow in hand, Thea and Irini both broke new ground. I stepped out of traditional middle-class American life and established my-self in Elika. There, the women and I have become a part of each other's cultural context; we help put each other's experiences into perspective. The women of Elika place pastoral life into perspective for me; I place "modern life" into perspective for them. The boundaries that might have limited our evolution stretch, reshape, dissolve—freeing us to expand into a wider realm. This realm is no longer confined by our own particular cultural heritage and biases. It is a realm limited only by our ability to see honestly and creatively and to act courageously. In my view, then, the Elikiotissa is not a fixed individual, but an individual in process. The name refers not to her destination, but to her journey.

The Elikiotissa is a woman who sings, on wing, the fundamental note that vibrates within.

initiation

In May 1990, I returned for the seventh time to a crop of wild wheat and stinging nettles growing inside my still roofless house. I wouldn't be able to enter, let alone get to work, without clearing out the invasion. And still I wouldn't be able to inhabit the house until I had restored a window and door opening, laid slate floors, and completed the interior walls. These jobs required removing original lintel beams without collapsing two meters of stone wall above, maneuvering slate slabs the size of sidewalk pavements, and fitting hundreds of chink stones into as many spaces in the walls.

I had only to complete this round of toil, and I would be moving into my house. But simply speaking, I did not feel up to it. By laboring in like manner for the previous six seasons, had I spent myself? Or was I too afraid to complete a monumental undertaking whose purpose remained a mystery? Certainly the book I went to Elika to write would be on paper before I would sweep the first winter's accumulation of soot from my chimney with a thyme-bush brush.

I purchased my house with the attitude that departures from it would never guarantee returns: political upheavals might shut me out, or personal matters might detain me. Consequently during restoration, I focused more on the process than the final outcome, and I found that I became completely absorbed and fulfilled by the most simple repetitious tasks: carrying brick, chinking walls. My efforts satisfied me even more when—from my work site—I could view the sea stretching gracefully toward her own misty horizon.

Over time, I became increasingly conscious that as I shaped my house, my house shaped me, or at least heightened my awareness of my "shape." I discovered, for example, my facility for invention—a capacity no doubt enhanced by the displays of ingenuity around me. Women set stones against the sides of loaves baking closest to the hot coals heaped by their oven doors to prevent that bread from charring while it baked. Olive pickers pin the edges of loosely woven plastic ground cloths together with twigs and anchor the cloths against the wind with stones; and to keep their seats dry when they stop for lunch, they sit on olive branches covered with empty burlap sacks. Plumbers bend pipes in the forks of trees. And farmers working alone prop one side of the packsaddle with a pole and load heavy cargo on the other side first—for balance.

Drawn on local resources, these common-sense practices have been imitated for generations. My house embodies my practical thinking, which I, too, implemented with materials at hand. When I needed five identically curved lengths of iron to reinforce the arched lintel over the window I cut in my kitchen wall, I could not achieve the required accuracy by using the conventional forked tree trunk. I bent the irons against an appropriately sized oil drum I spotted in Eleni's yard across the ravine.

When I built an eleven-meter form, which I used to pour a twenty-two-meter reinforced-concrete top ring for my roof, I used a wiring system I had developed doing smaller jobs. I worked *in situ* on top of the walls. Buffeted by hot August winds, I stood or stooped on a ledge narrower than the length of my shoe. The manual drill I used to cut wire holes required two hands to operate, so I employed one foot to prevent the wood I drilled from backing away from me. One time a neighbor man caught me—tired and sweaty—in the midst of this treachery. After a superficial inspection he announced authoritatively, "It won't do." Because unsolicited advice and unfounded forecasts of doom are commonplace in Greece, I usually ignore them. But this man's untimely, ill-mannered intrusion filled me with a sea of anger that I released on him, flood-like, lest his intolerance of innovative freedom diminish the self-satisfaction generated by my own inventive process.

I formed the top ring in 1989. Two years prior to that, in preparation for the ring, I leveled the tops of the walls by replacing stones that winters of rain had washed away. The work involved endless flights up and down an extension ladder. One day I was unusually thirsty. I drank water every time I descended the ladder, but still craved liquid. When I went to the village that afternoon, I learned what I had been too preoccupied to acknowledge—a heat wave had set in.

I had moved out of my first rental that year because tiles had blown off and the roof leaked. Like my first rental, my new place had no trees or grape arbor to shade verandas or interior rooms. But whereas the thick stone walls and clay tile roof of the first house moderated daytime highs, the concrete walls and roof of my new rental intensified them. Because temperatures during the heat wave peaked somewhere between one hundred ten and one hundred twenty degrees, work in the afternoon was unthinkable. And because the two scrawny olive trees at my own house provided negligible shade, I had to wait out the heat in my sun-baked rental.

There, I stripped off my clothes and lay on my bed. I was too hot to read or write. I was too hot to sleep. I was too hot to think. I was so hot I might as well have been stone cold. Like spirits rising from the dead, like smoke rising from the red-hot embers of an olivewood fire, I drifted. For three or four hours at a time, day after day for three weeks, I wandered. When the heat wave broke, I left for the States. When I returned to Elika the next spring, I neither created agendas nor evaluated progress. I simply worked and celebrated day by day. The heat wave had taught me patience. I had discovered the moment.

Every year of my restoration, I contended with sacks of cement which, at fifty kilos apiece, match my own one hundred ten pounds. But during the summer that I formed the top ring, I worked longest and hardest. From a ladder I raised the height of my one gabled wall. From a ladder I raised the height of my circular stone chimney. Then I formed and helped pour the concrete top ring. Afterward, from a ladder, I faced the interior of the top ring with stone. And finally, I carried, rolled, or walked floor slates from the road to my house. The work tested my strength and taxed my endurance. I slept deeply, and when I rose from bed each morning and afternoon, I shuffled on stiff ankles like an old woman.

After five months—two more than usual—I was ready to stop. I had met the limits of my physical endurance; I couldn't imagine working any longer.

At times it also seemed as if I had met the limits of my physical strength, which indeed felt mighty. When I climbed the ladder with a stone too big to handle or hand-bent concrete reinforcing irons too rigid to yield, my strength seemed unlimited. I attributed to the power of my will the fact that I always found the strength I needed. Perhaps it was Hercules.

As I look back on the restoration, I realize I do not know the person who undertook and accomplished the work. I do know the process—like childbearing—empowered me. In 1989 I boarded the plane for the States on October fifteenth, my birthday. I felt as if I were embarking on my own maiden voyage.

Although I feel less and less acquainted with the one who committed to reshaping the *mantri* into a house, I am increasingly familiar with the voice that dictated the purchase. At first I did not know I had access to the voice. I fitted stones by trial and error, and I made many mistakes.

During the work season, I had little company other than the surrounding stones. To excuse the slow improvement in my Greek, I often told the villagers, laughingly, that throughout the day I talked to the stones, but the stones did not talk back. Actually, it feels as if they did talk back. When I restored my doorway, I needed to face in stone the reinforced-concrete slab I had poured over the lintel beams. By that time, I had become attuned to the voice and listened for it. Throughout the entire job, the first stone I picked up always exactly suited the intended space over the door.

If I listen to it, the voice that demanded the *mantri* purchase and guided its restoration will also inform me when I must come home to the *mantri,* and when I must travel from it.

banner day

Two hours before sunset on September the fifth, 1990, Yiannis Grimbilas, master carpenter, cemented the final roof tile into place and declared the job complete. Before descending his ladder—whether for my benefit or for his own—he tipped a pail of water at the crest of the roof. As we watched the stream run down the grooves and trickle over the edge, we both clapped and cheered with childlike delight.

Grimbilas had promised to begin roofing my house on the fifteenth of June. After that, like a shadow in the summertime, I followed him persistently from job to job and urged him to roof my house next. At the same time, I completed the essential interior work at my house—floored the kitchen with slates from a torn-up threshing circle and pointed the walls. Grimbilas' "late" arrival on August twenty-seventh was, as I had anticipated, exactly on time; when the roof finally went on, I was ready to move in.

I had already set up a bed in the kitchen of my unfinished house; tucked into it, I could watch for shooting stars as I drifted off to sleep at night. As soon as the roof went on, I

moved in my bottled-gas cookstove and other kitchen equipment, including an ant-proof bread board I hung by ropes
from a crossbeam. I also moved in a table and chair and a
newly purchased portable brass kerosene-fueled lamp. I had
paid four hundred fifty dollars for an electric pole twelve
months earlier, but the electrician I hired to draw up the req-
uisite wiring plan failed to meet the submission deadline, and
a four- to six-month installation delay was extended indefinitely, it seemed. Despite lessons from my fisherman friend
Stathis, when I lit the lantern, it burst into temporary but
frightening flame. And the little smoke it produced filled the
room with a noxious smell.

Having equipped my house with the bare essentials—
because I still had no windows or doors—I set about my
reading and writing. After a return trip to Skopeles on foot, I
revised "Homing," which I had written in the spring. Then,
with my dictionary close at hand, I began the tedious process
of translating some interviews an Athenian friend had helped
me conduct with Thea in 1983, and I wrote "Maiden Voyage."
During the day when I looked up from my work, light beam-
ing through arched windows cut in my massive stone walls
drew my attention outside, across the threshing circle and
over the hilly olive groves to the mountainous seacoast and
islands offshore.

At night, my lamp dimly lit the bare stone walls and
rough-hewn roof timbers that surrounded me, and I read and
wrote safe as a monk in his chamber. When my eyes tired, I
crawled into bed.

I slapped mosquitoes throughout the night, and then I
woke to the sound of my neighbor Rinoula's staff tapping up
the rocky footpath alongside my house. (I was still sleeping in

my kitchen because I had not yet laid the other floor.) Rinoula did not have to be at the fields to work at daybreak in September, so she was free to make an early morning pilgrimage to Maravelianika's chapel, Ay Stratigos. The chapel sits on the hill several hundred meters above my house. During the years I worked on my house, I felt reassured by the chapel's presence, and I knew I would miss being able to view its dove-white facade from inside my house once it was roofed. This proved to be true, but now I could rely on Rinoula to relay my greetings, which I silently bestowed on her as she walked by.

As Rinoula wound her way past the ghosts of five houses above mine and then on up to the chapel, I pictured her short-cut dark curly hair, the apron still tied around her waist, and the plastic sandals and men's socks that protected her feet. I also listened to the birds twittering in the crowns of fig, citrus, and olive trees growing in the ravine between my house and Eleni's. When a faint tapping sound signaled Rinoula's return, I jumped out of bed, pulled my polo shirt over my head, buttoned the fly of my pleated khaki shorts, and leapt to my kitchen window in time to greet Rinoula before she disappeared from sight. She stopped only long enough to turn a sunny face toward me and wave her staff triumphantly in the air—we had both looked forward to the time we would become neighbors.

I took a break from house construction work after I moved in—the muscles I had taxed during the summer months whimpered while I was sitting still and yelped if I exerted myself. Instead, I hosted a friend from home, I hiked in the mountains, and I swam at Marathia. Each time I saw my house from a distance, I smiled at the sight of the red tile roof and my clean clothes dancing on the line stretched over my semicircular roof terrace. The display reminded me of a tradition Eleni had described to me when I was finishing the addition to my house a few years before. When master builders like Eleni's father finished constructing the walls of a house, they tied a colorful or white kerchief to a cord strung around the top rim of the walls. This banner invited family, neighbors, and friends to celebrate the completion of the house; they made gifts of kerchiefs, towels, and tablecloths which fluttered alongside the master builder's banner.

Of all the village traditions that have died, I wish most that this festival of color could be resurrected. When I moved into my house, Eleni and Rinoula each gave me a homemade rag rug. When I look into the vibrant red stripes crossing their now faded red warps, I can almost picture a host of inaugural banners waving at my house.

dreams and expectations

In September 1990, Greece was crippled by nationwide strikes in the civil services. Bank personnel initiated the strikes to protest new retirement regulations. Shortly after the banks closed, postal services terminated, and the electric company instituted daily unscheduled prolonged power blackouts.

By the time the strikes stopped at the end of the month, I had been living contentedly in my roofed house for three weeks. Wet weather was due any time, however, so I began to shadow my carpenter Barbayiannis in Neapolis. He had measured for my windows and door in May, but we had agreed to installing them after the house had been roofed. When I met him on the street on the twenty-seventh of September, I asked him, "When?" Because he simply shrugged and turned his attention elsewhere, I knew better than to press him. Departing summer vacationers had overwhelmed him with demands in August, and the power blackouts in September had set him further behind.

The weather turned cool on October fourth; bracing

winds swept through my open kitchen and stiffened my neck as I worked at my writing table. I called Barbayiannis from the telephone *cafenio*, and I made an appeal based on the necessity of fire in winter. I reminded him that until I saw how my chimney drew in a closed house, I could not finish building my hearth. He said he would cut the frames that afternoon. When I visited his shop a week later, no frames were in sight. "Everyone is yelling at me," he protested. "I'm not yelling at you," I gently noted. "No, you're not," he acknowledged. But he made no promises.

I woke up at three-thirty in the morning on October fifteenth, my birthday. The god Boreas had become angry; the north wind raged. Maniacally, it thundered through my open house and heaved my bed with me on it. I never returned to sleep. This wind was more rabid than most, and its sound and feel unnerved me. Promising not to return until my windows were installed, I abandoned my house at dawn.

I returned to my rental, a place where I had been making do since 1987. In spite of the fact that my second rental had serviceable windows and doors, my arrival was not a homecoming. Knowing from the start that my stay in that house would be temporary, I had personalized the place with nothing more than three small photographs I hung by my bed. The first was a picture I made while hiking unmaintained trails in the Grand Canyon; it captures the magic of the canyon at sunset. Another was a photograph of Castle, a homestead in the mountains above Eagle, Colorado. My friend Rita's grandparents built the cabin, whose simplicity inspires my lifestyle in Elika. The third was a portrait of five generations in my family. At age one, I sit on my mother's lap while my older sister sits beside us. My mother's father,

her grandfather, and his father stand at attention behind us. I believe I was born on my great-great-grandfather's one-hundredth birthday; he lived one hundred and four years.

Beyond this memorabilia, there was nothing appealing about the two-room rental. The concrete walls in the bedroom, kitchen, and bathroom dampened when it rained, and flakes of whitewash dropped on the floor faster than I could sweep them away. Throughout, the floors were bumpy bare concrete. Because the bathroom floor sloped uphill to a pencil-sized drain hole, showering was impossible. For the same reason, I had to be careful not to spill water on the floor when sponge-bathing.

The entry door opened into the kitchen, where I had placed my stove and refrigerator. Someone had torn out the old-style sink and installed a more beautiful terrazzo sink in a tiny outside room. It was easy enough to load up with vegetables from the crisper and get through the door to the outside sink to prepare a meal—the inside door handle turned easily with one hand. But getting back into the kitchen with an armful of clean pots and glassware after the wind had blown the door shut behind me was another matter—the key that opened the door from the outside required two hands to turn! To make matters worse, the kitchen sink drain was cracked; waste water gushed onto the floor under foot. And tomato seeds sprouted in pools of water trapped where the marble chips had eroded.

The fireplace was in the kitchen; it smoked. And I could not see out of the house. The door glass was textured, and the window shutters were too dilapidated to open. Luckily half the kitchen window shutter had fallen off, and I had a limited view of the neighbor's gate.

Once I returned to my rental, the conditions there spurred me to keep nudging Barbayiannis. At seven forty-five in the morning two days after I reinhabited it, I set out to hitchhike the half-hour drive to Neapolis. I thought the winds had finally died down, so I dressed lightly. But the winds picked up as the sun rose. Three rides and ninety minutes later, I arrived at the carpentry shop. I was chilled through and angry. I had missed Barbayiannis, who worked on site that day, by five minutes.

Two days later I had better luck hitching, and I found the carpenter at his shop. I thought perhaps I should try yelling at him Greek style, but even after the experience with the cold on the road two days previously, I didn't feel like it. Instead I considered the fact that Greek men tend to like rounded women. I explained to Barbayiannis that I had moved my cooking equipment into my own house, and I had had access only to cold food out of my refrigerator since my retreat to the rental. To dramatize my situation, I sucked in my stomach and pulled out the waist of my baggy trousers. "Look, I'm hungry," I said. "I'll have your windows in a week," he replied with the first smile I had seen in some time. "Certain?" I asked. "Certain," he answered. In Greece, that's a promise. I was thrilled. But when I called a week later to set an installation date, he stated unapologetically that he had not begun the job. When I asked for his revised schedule, he said, "We'll see."

October came and went. For weeks I had been prodding the carpenter to no avail. With each effort and failure, the number on the Richter scale measuring my frustration rose. It was not a question of patience. I was able to accept delays— although I was profoundly disappointed when I had to abandon my tranquil abode in Maravelianika. Fundamentally, it was a matter of trust; Barbayiannis said one thing and did another. Exasperating. Disheartening. Sometimes infuriating.

To maintain a sense of autonomy during the treasure hunting, I made every effort to deal with the carpenter's inconstancy when I felt most flexible and to focus wholeheartedly on other affairs the rest of the time. It happened to be, primarily, a time for writing.

All summer long, I had labored at my house. For six weeks during July and August, I had worked every day, ten to twelve hours a day, to finish the interior walls of the main room—a vast two-story space encompassing the original salon and stable below. I picked out old mud mortar, I mixed fresh cement mortar, I carried mortar and chink stones up as many as eleven steps on an extension ladder, and I tucked the stones and mortar into the spaces in the walls with a hammer and trowel or, more often, my fingers. At some point, I became conscious that this process drew on my masculine energy. Indeed, I had been impregnating the walls. This awareness triggered a desire for balance; I needed to be impregnated myself. At that time, a giant phallus appeared in a dream.

At the same time, the main room I was finishing took on the feeling of a spacious but empty womb. This awakened me to a feeling of expansion in my own womb. At age forty-five, I had entered the prime of my womanhood. I yearned to fulfill the essence of my femininity, but not through childbearing. I had already done that metaphorically when, two years earlier, I built my expectant chimney. I knew, instead, I would write.

This fact explains why I did not hesitate to resume writing *Dancing Girl*—which I had been working at off and on for two years—once my house was roofed and I moved in, and why I continued to write *Dancing Girl* when I returned to my rental. New stories gestated while I read pages of interviews with Thea, Mihail, and Irini; and shortly thereafter, I delivered them, one after another, swiftly and fearlessly: "Clear Vision," "Orphans," and "The Astronomer."

On November second, I interrupted my writing to look again for my windows. No luck. For the first time, I felt distraught. Then I recalled the image of a towering blue wave I had dreamed a few nights before. I saw the wave through the open door of a tiny dwelling something like my rental. The wave rose up so close to me, it seemed as if we might merge. It evoked not fear, but awe.

When I pictured the wave the second time, I realized that it represents my feminine energy—the creative energy I draw upon when I write. The dream reminded me how powerful and abundant my creative resources are, as the litter of recent stories proved. That afternoon, I dismissed my expectation to lay down in my own house, before leaving Elika for the winter, the rag rugs Eleni and Rinoula had given me. And that evening, by the safe and clean electric light in my rental, I wrote "Good News." The next morning, before climbing out of my midnight blue iron bed, I bore this story and "Banner Day."

halcyon days

On the morning of November the eighth, I confirmed by telephone that Barbayiannis had at long last made my door and window frames. I anticipated that he would finish the door itself, the sashes, screens, and shutters without further delay. Wanting the frames to be weatherproof when installed, I spent the eighth and the ninth tarring and oiling them at Barbayiannis' shop. The work satisfied me; each brush stroke carried me one step closer to home.

The next week, daytime temperatures inside my rental hovered around fifty degrees Fahrenheit, and every time a south wind blew, my rental fireplace belched smoke. The hot meals my Danish neighbor Lisbeth brought me were a welcome change from cold food out of my refrigerator, but I nevertheless began to contract in the cold.

After a week, I returned to my carpenter. My frames still stood empty. For the first time, with a surge of emotion, I told Barbayiannis that his indifference deprived me of the satisfaction of living in a house I had worked by myself for seven years to fix. "Excuse me," I said, "but I must tell you. You have spoken only lies from the beginning." He looked me in the eye. "You have justice," he admitted. "I still love you," I continued, "but I need more firewood. I don't know where to deliver it." I detected sadness in his eyes. "Deliver it to your house," he said resolutely. "Your windows and door will be ready next week." That was November the fourteenth.

Drizzly weather set in, and indoor temperatures dropped to the low forties. I donned more clothes and wrote more stories. And I laid the floor of my house's main room. Christmas came and went. At Zoe's on New Year's Eve, I saw Kyriakos' wife Hariklia. Since Kyriakos' death the previous year, Hariklia had been despondent and introspective. "Kyriakos always said, 'Let's go see what Thordis is doing at her house.' He loved you," she told me. "I never came," she said, "but I used to go to your house when I was young. I was the fifth child in my family and I was so energetic, my parents told me I was not their child—they said they took me from the gypsies. I didn't understand. I worried. I hid at your house and found peace."

By mid-January my door, windows, screens, and shutters were ready. Barbayiannis had promised to deliver them on the seventeenth, but by mid-morning he had not appeared. When I called, he said, "It's too cold. I'll come on Saturday."

On Saturday Barbayiannis arrived. We tried to set the frames in the openings. Not one frame fit. As we chiseled away stone to make room, I said, "I'm glad for me that the window frames you measured do not fit since the door frame I measured does not fit."

In a few hours, all the frames had been installed and the

door, sashes, screens, and shutters had been hung. I tried to close one of the screens. It did not close against its stop, and I could foresee mosquitoes and flies buzzing freely into the house. "Why?" I asked Barbayiannis. He said the shutters would not come out if the screens closed against the stop. Then I closed one of the shutters. It sprang on its hinges. "Look!" I exclaimed. "It doesn't matter," he answered. Then I noticed that the miter joints in the sashes were not filled. "I'm not good with plastic wood," I said. "Leave it; it's better that way," he gibed. He packed his tools and left me. "I'll pay you on Monday," I called after him.

I spent the next week oiling my door and windows and attaching locks after I filled miter joints and reseated hinges. (At the same time, Elika's licensed electrician skillfully wired my house. But he could not hook it up because although the hole had been dug in mid-November, the electric pole I had paid for more than a year before had not been delivered.) Finally I went to Barbayiannis. "I'm a week late," I acknowledged. "You need wood," he teased. I pictured my carpenter brandishing a staff as I handed him a hinge that had been broken when an impatient apprentice forced it into place with a hammer. "No," I replied, "your apprentice needs wood. I had to reseat many of the hinges." When I told him the shutters work fine when the screens close against the stop, he looked surprised.

"I didn't come until I was sure I could fix everything," I said reprovingly. "The window you cut in my door is not acceptable. I'm willing to pay another carpenter to remake it when I return." "No, bring it to me. I'll do it," he said. "The door and windows did not arrive late," I said, "but all the repair work has been a nuisance. I'd be furious if I had not been able to accomplish it. It's lucky I have the tools." "And the skill," he added. "If I need some money next year, I'll come work for you." "All right," he replied. "I feel as if it is still good between us," I added. "Yes," he agreed. "None of the frames fit," I reminded him. "Even so, when you chiseled the stone, you worked with joy," I explained. The halcyon spirit that presided over my house in Hariklia's youth abides there still, I thought. I paid Barbayiannis, who charged me fairly, considering, and we bade each other farewell.

Two days later, I moved into my house. That afternoon, I danced on the beach. That evening, I visited Irini. She knew me. I told her I would be leaving the next day. She understood; she asked me when I would return.

That night I made up a bed at my house. I slept a stormless sleep. In the morning from my lookout, I witnessed sky, sea, and village. During the day, I packed my bags, and that afternoon, I boarded the bus for Athina. Two days later, I flew across the Atlantic.

I had been in Elika for nine months. Even though my core felt as sturdy as the original century-old lintel beams that continue to hold up the walls at my house, the transition back to the States was a difficult one. On the airplane, I traveled mutely. For the duration of my time in Elika, my reality had the quality of a dream, and I feared that the first words spoken in English would, like Thor's thunder, wrench me from slumber.

The day after I arrived in Denver, I went for a walk and ended up at a shopping mall where I drifted aimlessly in a sea of consumer goods. Day after day, I woke in the morning with no sense of where I was. And day after day, I saw only blindly. "Which is better," the villagers often ask me, "Greece or America?" "Neither is better; they are different," I always reply. But during my transition days, when the question crossed my mind, I had no answer. I simply yearned for more halcyon days.

patina

A patina glosses the handle of Spiros' wild-olivewood plowstock. I can't say what the patina represents to him: drudgery, perhaps resentment, indifference, satisfaction, maybe exhilaration—probably a blend of these. I do know that at age sixty-six, Spiros' physique and laughter are robust, he relates amicably to his team, and he welcomed my company the morning we spent together.

I intended that day to make photographs of the olive harvest. I had turned off the main road at Stratis' auto repair garage and was headed along an agricultural road toward Marathia when Spiros overtook me on his donkey. The plow roped to the packsaddle on his horse caught my eye, and I asked if I could follow along and make photographs. "Come," he said, so I fell in.

Before we had gone two hundred meters, I noticed a village woman by an olive tree just off the road. An unpainted wooden ladder with widely spaced rungs towered over her as she walked it around the tree. Exactly the photograph I was hoping for! Turning toward her, I abandoned Spiros without a word of warning.

As I approached the woman, she parted brittle branches with the top of her ladder without breaking them and set it against a sturdy limb. When I presented myself to her, she had already climbed the ladder and had resumed her sawing. Freshly cut branches piled up under the tree had told me she was pruning.

While I waited for her to descend again and relocate her ladder so I could record her relationship to it on film, I sat on a small stone in a plowed area where tender green spears of winter-sown oats shot up from the furrowed earth toward a blue-and-white picture-puzzle sky, and I marveled at the inimitable beauty of the shadow of olive leaves cast by the sun on the woman's plain sand-colored skirt. I had been working, isolated, at my writing table for several days, and this reintroduction to my surroundings, like the taste of thyme honey, was beginning to intoxicate me.

When I finished photographing the woman with her ladder, I told her I had lost Spiros. She said I would find him working at a low place farther down where the road forks. I knew I needed no directions, however; his commands to his plow team would locate him.

Sure enough, before I spotted two packsaddles sitting unused for the moment by the edge of the field where Spiros plowed, I heard, "Slow, Girl! Back! Fuck your wedding papers!" When I recognized the plowman's voice, I smiled the knowing smile that crosses my face when a rattling sound tells me someone is knocking almonds from a tree with a staff, and when I hear plunking sounds and know plowed-up potatoes are being collected in old lard tins. Life on the land speaks its own language. It is my mother tongue.

When I found Spiros, he had already tilled the soil under the boughs of one olive tree, and he was cultivating around another. I could see he was his own master: he drank when he was thirsty, he ate when he was hungry, and he rested when he was tired. And when he worked, he laid down as many furrows as he wanted, where he wanted, in the direction and at the rate he determined.

My life in Elika is dramatically different from Spiros', and even from his wife Matina's, who could more easily be seen as my counterpart. When I passed her house on my way home from the field at noon, I told her Spiros was asking for the fresh shirt he had forgotten, and I knew she would carry it to him on foot. Spiros tells the story of one life when he scribes the land with his plow; his wife Matina would record a different story on the lines he scribes; and I write yet another.

I write about my own autonomy in Elika. I work on my house, write, photograph, hike, pay social calls, work for hire and to help, eat, and sleep—all under the auspices of Ay Stratigos—as the spirit moves. I write about the richness of my surroundings: resinated wine perfuming the streets in September, the stabbing red color of bougainvillea blossoms year round, the mournful call of the cuckoo bird at night.

I write of my indelible friendships: children call me from the school yard, and I wave back; Rinoula brings coffee to workers at my house, and I take her the first melon of the season; Papoulis calls me his first cousin from America, and I almost always purchase my hardware from his store in Neapolis.

I write of the ability of Elika to inspire: the centering power of the threshing circle, the mystery of the spirits inhabiting the olive trees, and the transforming power of the dark starlit night.

And I write of the plowed earth: how soft the moist fresh-tilled soil feels underfoot and how rich its fragrance; and under force of the plowshare, how the earth rises up in waves even more inspiring than the ones we paint in our dreams.

I can't explain why I first came to Elika. But I can explain why I return. I return to touch the patina on the handle of Spiros' plow.

About the Author

Thordis Simonsen designed and taught high school courses in biology and anthropology for fifteen years. Currently she works as a free-lance writer, visual artist, and guest speaker. Through readings, discussion, and slide illustrations, Thordis' presentations of her first book, *You May Plow Here: The Narrative of Sara Brooks*, have engaged high school and university audiences as far away as Stavanger, Norway. Her photographic portrait of Alabama mule farming in the 1970s has been exhibited in galleries from Colorado to New York. Thordis resides alternately in Elika, Greece, and Denver, Colorado.

Praise for
You May Plow Here: The Narrative of Sara Brooks
edited by Thordis Simonsen

"A powerful story of survival that will live for generations."
—*The San Francisco Chronicle*

"A joy and revelation. . . . A story about immense courage, faith and spirit."
—*The Washington Post*

"You don't just read *You May Plow Here*, you listen to it. Brooks' vivid pictorial memory allows her to conjure up scenes from 70 years ago as though they had occurred an hour ago."
—*The Denver Post*

"Now we have a woman's narrative to stand alongside those of Nate Shaw and Hosea Hudson. I found the description of farm life unusually evocative; the narrator's 'voice' distinctive, consistent, and a lift to the spirit; the story of marriage and work life honest and human. The photographs are outstanding."
—*Jacquelyn Hall, Director*
Southern Oral History Program
The University of North Carolina

"A prideful, joyful outpouring. . . . To read *You May Plow Here* is not so much to read a book as to meet a woman of exceptional character. . . . This book fits neatly onto the shelf of what the author Alice Walker calls 'womanist prose.'"
—*Best Sellers*

"Longtime friend Simonsen edited her tapes of Brooks so sensitively that there is little distance between reader and storyteller; she activates voice on the printed page in much the same way author Studs Terkel did in his book *Working*."
—*Seattle Post–Intelligence*